I0176857

BEYOND REASON

BEYOND REASON

BY

HEATHER FREYSDOTTIR

BURNING HEART PRESS

BEYOND REASON

Published by Burning Heart Press, Copyright © 2015 by Heather Freysdottir. All rights reserved. No part of this publication may be reproduced, stored in a retrieval system, or transmitted in any form or by any means, electronic, mechanical, recording or otherwise, without the prior written permission of the author.

Manufactured in the United States of America

For more about Heather, visit http://heatherfreysdottir.com/

Visit Burning Heart Press at http://burningheartpress.com/
Cover art © 2015 by Dagulf Loptson

ISBN-10 0-9787401-4-9
ISBN-13 978-0-9787401-4-6

CONTENTS

DEDICATION AND THANKS

To my Beloved Loki, Who wouldn't let me avoid writing this book. To my wife, for her penchant for bullhorn motivational speeches. Much gratitude is in order for my beta readers and editor, for letting me vent while I struggled with the direction of the book, and with what to share and what to keep silent.

Much love and thanks to Hunters Kith and Kin – I wouldn't be brave enough to write this without your love and support. I'm fortunate to be doing this Work with brilliant minds and devoted hearts. You are the very best kindred any witch could ask for, and I love you all. Finally, many thanks to my ancestors, for their love and guidance. Hail the Beloved Dead!

BEYOND REASON

by

Heather Freysdottir

A Note On Capital Pronouns

Deity names and pronouns are capitalized to indicate Who they belong to in a sentence, and also because yours truly considers it polite to acknowledge Loki's Godhood. Occasionally He's been known to desire me to capitalize human pronouns as well, to acknowledge the Divine in all of us. If a "they" or an "us" is capitalized, it reflects that Divinity.

PART I: ONCE UPON A WITCH

(because our feet will put us on the right path, even when we are unaware)

MERRY MEET

This is a book about Loki, and His worship by a modern-day practitioner. It is not a book on reconstructionism or Heathenry. Worshipping Loki in those contexts is just as valid as what I'm writing about here, but since it's not my form of worship, I will leave it to someone better suited than myself. There is a dearth of information on Loki's historical cultus, however, if you're looking to worship Him in a Heathen context, there are resources, including, but not limited to, Neil Price's *The Viking World*, or The Troth's *Idunna* #93 (Fall 2012), which contains Kveldúlfr Gundarsson's essays, "Loki's Role in the Northern Religions." Even if you're not interested in worshipping Loki in a heathen context, Gundarsson's essays are a fascinating look into Loki's character.

Is This a Godspouse Book?

It's a book by a godspouse, and it's about my experiences with Loki. A general book about godspousery has been considered by many, and some more experienced than me, but no one has ever finished one, because godspousery is a type of mysticism, and by its nature is varied and highly individualistic. Take what is useful of my experiences, leave aside what isn't, and don't be afraid if your experiences or conclusions are different than mine. My words are a jumping off point for your own explorations; they are not the law.

So if you're reading this and trying to figure out "how do I do mysticism??", I'm sharing some of my experiences with Loki, in the hopes that you'll read it with the understanding that things can vary wildly from Deity to Deity, spouse to spouse – and even though I'm using "Deity," there are people who are wed to Spirits that aren't named in any particular Lore, or who aren't otherwise named Deities.

Now that I've mentioned that experiences vary, I'd like to talk about some of the commonalities that many spouses have – and again, keep in mind that any given relationship may have some of these but not all, and that doesn't negate the relationship:

- An intense, aching desire for the Beloved

- The relationship is about love – often about the spouse learning to love themselves and to see themselves through their Beloved's eyes

- Many give some sort of service to their Beloved, and that varies based on what the individual is good at – some it's just a personal devotional practice and self-development, some are priests or priestesses, some do lots of astral work, some serve their local communities in their Beloved's name in some other aspect that honors Them.

- Many spouses find that their relationship with their Beloved goes back further than they realized in some fashion.

- Many are knowledgeable about their Beloved, and may know about their historical worship; however, not all are

Polytheists or Reconstructionists.

- There is usually a sexual or ecstatic component to the relationship, and often both are present.

- Relationships between a Beloved and their spouse may involve intense, and sometimes conflicting emotions on both Their parts.

- If a Deity or Spirit has many aspects, the spouse may interact with one or more of those aspects more often than others. For example, in my own relationship with Loki, I interact with the Gift-Giver aspect of Himself far more often than the Breaker of Worlds.

- Shared Daily Life: what that looks like can vary tremendously, but in general, the Beloved is present in their spouse's life. This may come across in a more or less formal way – Loki, for example, isn't terribly formal, and He very much enjoys the magic of everyday life. Other examples might be daily offerings or meditations, but often, it is the spouse's daily routine shared between Them.

That's a brief overview of some basics, and again, people's experiences of the Divine do vary, and should, so if you're reading this and being pulled into mysticism or a devotional relationship, don't be afraid to explore the places your Beloved will take you. Some of them are the most joyous and ecstatic experiences you'll ever have; others might be terrifying, and that brings me to discussing what I mean by "terrifying."

What is terrifying? Well, that depends on who you are. For

me, it was terrifying to discover that my Muse was Someone and not just a construct in my head or an egregore, but a Power with His own notions of what w/We ought to be doing. The notion of sexual vulnerability terrifies one spiritworker friend of mine. Another could do or at least try damn near anything sexually, but finds being emotionally vulnerable absolutely terrifying.

And those types of things will probably not be relegated to one sole area – for example, I am a very private person, and I fought Loki for a long time about writing this. I am extroverted enough that I enjoy working with people, but working with people and enjoying talking about myself are not the same thing. I offer up this example just to say that in my own experience, Loki asks me to do things that I can handle, but are not necessarily in my comfort zone.

And how do you even know if you've heard correctly? I have some basic rules of thumb:

Is what you heard fawningly praising? Probably not heard correctly. Usually a Spirit will be honest with you about your strengths and weaknesses. Some are more blunt than others.

Is what you heard overwhelmingly negative? Note: this does not mean that a Power will never criticize you, but it does mean that the Power will say something that you recognize as legitimate. That often comes in the form of shadow work, which I will talk about more later on in this book. Another thing that is probably not a legitimate communication is, "I love so and so more than you." People can and do have negative self-talk, and this is the type that undermines your relationship with your Beloved.

Does whatever you heard serve your best interests? For

example, a Power shouldn't be asking you to jump off a bridge literally; if you're being asked to move cross-country, They will find a way to get you there. It may not magically appear, but They should have a plan of making the goal achievable. When Loki asked me to leave my mortal spouse, I had no income and I was quite ill, but within hours of the request, a safe home had been secured for my child and me. That said, if you think that the communication is legitimate, and you still have misgivings, than you have the right to discuss that with Them at more length. A Being with your best interests at heart will allow you to negotiate; some will even negotiate with your ancestors in order to achieve something.

I'll add a caveat to this, because I know that some Deities are more flexible than others – Loki, for example, responds infinitely better to negotiation than if He asks something and I refuse. If Odin asks me to do a thing, I rarely get an explanation of why, and once when I was balking at a task, He said to me, "why do you think it's optional?" That said, it was a task that I could complete, I just didn't want to at the time.

If it's a request, is it one that you can and should fulfill? For example, sometimes a Deity will ask you to gift something to a person, but it should be something that is within your means – Loki's asked me to gift people with books, jewelry, etc, but nothing that would have bankrupted me.

Does what you heard sound reasonable? For example, if I heard, "Write a book of poetry," I would consider that a reasonable request. If I heard "write a book about sharks," I would probably think I'd misheard that – there are other people who are more knowledgeable about that subject and who would do a better job at it.

Why Me?

I asked myself this a *lot*. It's not an easy question to answer in some ways, because I don't know why people are chosen by Them. Spiritworkers, including godspouses, come from all walks of life, from writers like myself, to teachers, parents, scientists, custodians, professors, secretaries, architects, engineers, and probably any other profession you can think of, there's someone who's god-touched in it, somewhere. When this all began, I was a lapsed Pagan, and borderline agnostic to atheist, so I was bewildered why I'd be chosen for anything spiritual.

Granted, I was not new to Paganism, but I'd never given spirituality or spiritual leadership any thought at all. I'd never desired to be a high priestess of a coven. I was a-ok with being a lay Pagan. When Loki initially asked me to write this book, I thought He meant a how-to, but really there is no how-to, because relationships with the Divine, even those that identify as godspouses, vary so much that I don't know if a how-to is really possible to attempt. I told Him as much, and so He said to me that I should write the story of Us instead.

In some ways that's easier and in some it's worse; I'm private, and it took Him a while to convince me to consider it, let alone write any of it down. So as you read, please consider that this is the story of Him and me, and a not primer on how to be a godspouse, or on what your devotional relationship should look like. If you find some elements useful, that's great, but I urge you to explore on your own. Peer corroboration can be wonderfully helpful but it's not a substitute for direct interaction with the

Holy Powers, and I would urge you to look to your Beloved before any other human authority. The joys of Paganism and Heathenry are that you are not bound to a central authority, save that of the Gods and ancestors. I hope that this story will encourage you to find your own voice, whether it is like mine or not.

Finally, I hope in talking about my life with Loki that people will gain some insight about why He is so loved by many, despite being feared by many as well – He is a loving God to His people, from the very casual lay devotee to the most ardent spouse. His path is as individual as the person walking it, and the places He leads you are unexpected, exhilarating, and often terrifying and beautiful.

Loki's appearance in my life took my preconceived notions about the distance between Gods and humanity, ripped them into shreds, set 'em on fire, and then He whizzed on the ashes. What? Mystic? Me? Mysticism is something that happens to someone else! In addition to that brain breakage, He revealed that He wasn't just lurking the actual story that we'd been writing, He was THE Muse.

I don't know how I didn't put that together on my own, either – I'd always had a sense that my Muse was the same underlying Thing no matter what His character looked like, but it took Him changing His appearance and me screaming and flailing for that insight to sink in. I loved my Muse – what writer doesn't? But it was such a shock to my system to perceive Him as something outside of me, a loss almost, as if part of me had been ripped away and replaced with this terrifying, awe-inspiring God Who had a bevy of wives and followers and who knew Him but

I didn't know any of them. It was a bit like being courted by a famous person, not knowing they were famous, and then going home at last and finding the crowds and paparazzi all screaming on His doorstep.

There was a definite element of DO NOT WANT. It was a horrid realization, because it wasn't as if I truly wanted Him to have a following of one, but I'd never wanted to be involved with Heathenry in any fashion; I wasn't a Reconstructionist Pagan, and it wasn't part of my religious practice. They weren't bad or anything, but the worldview was so very different from my own that there was a double culture shock. One of getting used to the ways in which Old Gods are just not human, and the human culture that worships Them, because recon and recon-derived traditions are very different from general eclectic Paganism in their in view.

And I felt spied on. He didn't do it out of spite, of course, and They take whatever opening that you give Them, mine just happened to be writing, but I felt betrayed and angry and I held Him at arm's length, which made Him hurt and frustrated. And none of that even addresses the amount of "help I am losing my marbles and He won't stop talking to me HELP" that also ran through my head off and on, because I think questioning your sanity is a rational response to all that if you've grown up in modern western society.

Clearly, however, I was now strapped into the Lokicoaster and not getting off the ride. I managed to work up the nerve to tell a friend – Stacy[1], my co-author that I wrote romantic fiction with, because she knew something was up and that I wasn't

---

1   Not their real name, for privacy reasons.

myself.

Fortunately for me, her response was wonderful. She took out a bottle of good scotch, flown home from a visit to Scotland, poured off a shot for Loki, another for herself, saluted our nuptials, and left the bottle out overnight. Loki, ever grateful, took the entire bottle and left the shot behind. She found the sealed, empty bottle three years later, so the first friend I told was also the first friend to utter, "Loki, You little shit!"

I told D², and they asked me what I wanted to get out of the relationship.

"Um, Loki?"

"I'm serious, Heather. What do you want Him to teach you?"

I had no answer. What did I want? Just Him. This is not to say that Loki hasn't given me gifts, because He has, but they aren't why I wanted Him. And ultimately, maybe that is why me? Or why any of us.

---

2   Privacy protected.

ABOUT THE PROVERBIAL GODPHONE

If you're unfamiliar with the term "godphone," you're not alone. I had never heard it until Loki. Godphone is a tongue-in-cheek nickname for communications with the Divine. This can range from hearing Spirit voices, to understanding that pops into a person's mind, to touch sensations, clairvoyance, tastes, and smells. Whether having a godphone is an innate or learned thing is a matter of debate in the Pagan mystical community. My ability to communicate with Loki came from writing with Him, so I can't definitively say whether I always had one or if nine years' of writing developed it. I do think that regardless of where you start out, practice can help a person learn some form of communication with Deity. There is a certain school of people who are of the attitude that a person should always second guess their UPG. I find that attitude demeaning and that telling someone to disbelieve all their UPG is to undermine their trust and relationship in the Divine. I know that the people who say this mean well, but the road to discernment is not paved with believe it all or believe none of it. And in regards to this, let me tell you about a dream I had. I was at a spirit worker school where everyone was handed out adult diapers. "Put 'em on, you're gonna need 'em."

"I don't understand why we need these...I mean, won't they be uncomfortable? And for number two, it'll be even worse... why do we need to infantilize ourselves for this Work?"

But of course, that was the point of the dream. Oh, Loki, making His point with diapers.

So how do I know that I've heard Them correctly?

To be very bluntly honest, I'd like to kill that question with fire. The pressure to have "right" UPG or to have heard Them right or somehow you're a crap *spiritworker/devotee/your relationship here* is bullshit. To me, hearing "right" is a very different thing than discernment. Asking yourself *why am I having this experience?* is an infinitely more productive question. An example:

- Step 1: Thought about X.
- - Discernment process – Is this a persistent thought? Give it time to come up again. If it does, go to Step 2. If not, Go to Step 1b.
- Step 1b. Let it go; it's a whim (yours or Theirs) or a blip in the godphone. Either way, don't dwell on it. Let it go.
- Step 2. It's persistent. Okay, take it seriously.
- Discernment process: does it come from Them or me?
- Step 2a. Does this (possible) UPG in some way self-aggrandize me? Or does it, in some way, reinforce negative things that I think about myself that allow me to self-sabotage? If no, proceed to Step 3. If yes, proceed to Step 2b.
- Step 2b. Yes, it does. Do NOT discard this persistent thought. This is the time to reach out to someone else if you find that this thought is beyond your ability to self-care. It's not a weakness to seek counseling, particularly if you are engaging in self-sabotaging behaviors. In the past year, I've been seeing a hypnotherapist off and on as

needed to work through my own shit. It's not weakness, but rather strength to take care of yourself. Some personal issues are beyond the scope of just chatting with a friend or fellow devotee. Go forth and heal thyself if you need to do that. It's no different than getting physical therapy for rehab after an accident. And certainly mental health issues don't preclude you from having a good godphone; Del Tashlin, author of the blog *Sex, Gods, and Rockstars* has written some excellent entries[3] on his dealing with having both.

- Step 3. No, this thought does not give me secondary gains of grandeur or sabotage. It's UPG. Go with your UPG. Learn to trust yourself.

- Caveat: if you feel you cannot be impartial about your UPG, even after sitting with it a while, then perhaps it's time to see an intercessory. Intercessories can consist of things like rune or tarot readings, oracles, seidhr, or possessory work. Even if you do seek an intercessory, keep in mind that everyone, including you, has their own personal experiences that may filter how the information comes through.

---

3   To view Del Tashlin's work on this subject, visit https://sex-godsrockstars.wordpress.com/tag/mental-illness/

GIDDYUP: ON HORSING AND POSSESSORY WORK

Possessory work is a tricky beast, and it's been written about by people who are more experienced than me, so I'm going to cover it briefly here. I'll include references in case you gentle readers want more in-depth information.

If you have suspicions or concerns about the authenticity of a possessory experience, you can arrange to have a password between yourself and your Beloved. It's a good failsafe if you're hearing things that don't sound like Them to you. Choose something that is shared only between the two of you. As with any other intercessory work, trust your gut – you can always get a second opinion, sit with it, or ask for a sign or omen to either back up or refute what was passed on to you.

So what is it like to see Loki in the flesh? It depends on who's housing Him, to some extent. The first time it happened, I was very giddy and girly. It was like meeting a rock star.

People also ask me other things about possession and meeting deities. Once, I had someone ask me if Loki could read their mind. It's kind of a yes and no answer. Most polytheists will tell you that our deities are not omniscient or omnipotent, and that's true. So can Loki read my mind? Or your mind? Sometimes. But the impression that I get is that it's invasive and that he would prefer not to engage in invasive behavior and so it is infinitely simpler for someone to tell him what they need or want. It's kind of the reverse when someone wonders about horsing, and whether or not the horse knows things that only the Deity could know. I can say this: sometimes the horse having a background schema helps. The best example I can give is that once he had possessed someone, and he was trying to communicate our personal codeword, and the horse didn't know that word because that word is in a dead language, and one that the horse had never heard of, and since Loki could not get them to say the word, he got the horse to say the English translation of the word, and then the name of the language. It was enough for me to know that he was in there even if he couldn't quite communicate the way he normally does when he's a discorporeal being.

ONCE A WITCH, ALWAYS A WITCH

Fall, 1987

I live in a tiny town deep in the swamps of Louisiana, in fishing territory. Jean Lafitte National Park is across the street from my house. We're new in the tiny town; previously we lived in the suburbs of New Orleans, and now we live in deep Cajun country. My new friends have grandparents that still speak French. "Anglais," a local declares my father and me. But my dad never met a stranger, and before long, he is working Bernard's shrimp boat on weekends and he has our neighbor on with him at the shipyard.

The swamp is dense and alive; I'm told not to go into it too deep alone. "Because of the gators?"

"No, chere, because of le loup garou. Dem woods full of haints; dey follow you home."

As a prudent child, instead of wandering in the swamp, I climb a path of oyster shells up the levee, bleached white from the sun, and look out on the bayou. It's quiet and peaceful here. I listen to the swamp, and it listens back to me. It's my retreat from middle school, from missing my old school, my old friends. On the other side of the Intercoastal waterway, a cemetery sits, its above ground family graves visible even from the bank. Come Halloween, I sit and watch people bring food and drink and lay it on their ancestors' graves. No le loup garou comes to bother me, although some nights I fancy I can hear howling in the swamp.

I make new friends. One of them is Kellie, and she has a spirit in her house, she says. "We've even had it exorcised and he won't leave."

Kellie's house is pretty and bright, and I don't feel afraid, so I spend the night. We do typical things – hair, makeup; spirit conjuring is part and parcel of sleepover party games. Bloody Mary, stiff as a board, light as a feather, and then we decide to see if we can sense our own auras. I take my hands and hold them apart about a foot. "Now, move them together until you can feel just a little resistance."

At about six inches in, I begin to feel a subtle resistance. A flicker of movement catches my eye, off in the corner. I see a figure – masculine in shape, and his face is scarred.

"You saw him too, didn't you?"

We stop playing our game. That night, we sleep in the same bed, covers pulled tight. He visits me in my dreams anyway, and I run from him. The next day, I tell my parents nothing, lest they decide not to let me visit with Kellie anymore.

The man with the scarred face comes to me in a dream that night too; I'm walking down the road between Kellie's house and mine and he walks behind me.

Dem woods full of haints; dey follow you home.

CONVERSION

Summer, 1992

My family lives in Florida now, and I'm in high school. My friend Anne has a Ouija board and a big blue book – *Buckland's Complete Book of Witchcraft*. Our friend Dara is with us, and even though she's an avowed atheist, she plays along. We talked to Something or Someone, but this time it didn't follow me home. I'm fascinated by Anna's big blue book, however, and I tell them both that if I'm ever not a Christian, I'd like to be a Pagan. My family is Christian, however, and so I don't make any abrupt moves to convert. The only Pagan person I know of anywhere is Anna, until I hit college.

I'm in the library, doing research for a paper. It's 1999, and in the part of Florida where I dwell, the information superhighway is more of a dirt road, so research is mostly paper-based, augmented with a computer bought on student loans. A book in the corner of the library catches my eye, *How the Irish Saved Civilization*. My grandma's family, the Donleys, are of Irish descent. Curious, I pick it up and start reading. Thomas Cahill's book is all about the Irish tradition of poetry and literacy, starting back with the Pagan poem known as the *Tain Bo Cuailnge*, or the *Cattle Raid of Cooley*. Intrigued, I pick up a copy of the *Tain*. It opens with this passage:

> "**ONCE** when the royal bed was laid out for Ailill and Medb in Cruachan fort in Connacht, they had this talk on the pillows:

'It is true what they say, love,' Ailill said, 'it is well for the wife of a wealthy man.'

'True enough,' the woman said. 'What put that in your mind?'

'It struck me,' Ailill said, 'how much better off you are today than the day I married you.'

'I was well enough off without you,' Medb said.

'Then your wealth was something I didn't know or hear much about,' Ailill said. 'Except for your woman's things, and the neighbouring enemies making off with loot and plunder.'

'Not at all,' Medb said, 'but with the high king of Ireland for my father — Eochaid Feidlech the steadfast, the son of Finn, the son of Finnoman, the son of Finnen, the son of Finngoll, the son of Roth, the son of Rigéon. the son of Blathacht, the son of Beothacht, the son of Enna Agnech, the son of Aengus Turbech. He had six daughters: Derbriu, Ethne, Ele, Clothru, Muguin, and myself Medb, the highest and haughtiest of them. I outdid them in grace and giving and battle and warlike combat. I had fifteen hundred soldiers in my royal pay, all exiles' sons, and the same number of freeborn native men, and for every paid soldier I had ten more men, and nine more, and eight, and seven, and six, and five, and four, and three, and two, and one. And that was only our ordinary household.

'My father gave me a whole province of Ireland, this province ruled from Cruachan, which is why I am called "Medb of Cruachan." And they came from Finn

the king of Leinster, Rus Ruad's son, to woo me, and
from Coirpre Niafer the king of Temair, another of Rus
Ruad's sons. They came from Conchobor, king of Ulster,
son of Fachtna, and they came from Eochaid Bee, and I
wouldn't go. For I asked a harder wedding gift than any
woman ever asked before from a man in Ireland — the
absence of meanness and jealousy and fear.

'If I married a mean man our union would be wrong,
because I'm so full of grace and giving. It would be an
insult if I were more generous than my husband, but not
if the two of us were equal in this. If my husband was a
timid man our union would be just as wrong because I
thrive, myself, on all kinds of trouble. It is an insult for
a wife to be more spirited than her husband, but not if
the two are equally spirited. If I married a jealous man
that would be wrong, too: I never had one man without
another waiting in his shadow. So I got the kind of man
I wanted: Rus Ruad's other son — yourself, Ailill, from
Leinster. You aren't greedy or jealous or sluggish. When
we were promised, I brought you the best wedding gift
a bride can bring: apparel enough for a dozen men, a
chariot worth thrice seven bondmaids, the width of your
face of red gold and the weight of your left arm of light
gold. So, if anyone causes you shame or upset or trouble,
the right to compensation is mine,' Medb said, 'for you're
a kept man.'" (trans. Kinsella)

Medb fascinates me. She is no man's possession; She is a
Queen in Her own right, and even a Kingmaker. She's sexual,
proud – haughty, by Her own admission – and unafraid to assert

Her desires, whether for wealth or pleasure. She is a "massive figure" completely and utterly unlike anything in the Christian worldview.

'Examine me,' Cethern said. 'This great wound here looks grave. What made it?'

'A vain, arrogant woman gave you that wound,' Fingin said.

'I believe you are right,' Cethern said. 'A tall, fair, longfaced woman with soft features came at me. She had a head of yellow hair, and two gold birds on her shoulders. She wore a purple cloak folded about her, with five hands' breadth of gold on her back. She carried a light, stinging, sharpedged lance in her hand,and she held an iron sword with a woman's grip over her head— a massive figure. It was she who came against me first.'

'Then I'm sorry for you,' Cúchulainn said. 'That was Medb of Cruachan.'

There is nothing in my birth religion comparable to Medb. I realize that Christianity feels flat to me. Religion is supposed to bring comfort in need, joy in good times. I have none of this, but I feel joy in Medb's exploits. Good, bad, She is Herself, and it is time for me to be Myself. I began to do research on Paganism. My son is a toddler, and I live with my parents, because I can't afford college without their help, mostly in the form of childcare and stable shelter. Come graduation, I sit down to pray to Team Christ. It's Lughnasadh – "Lord, I think I want to be a Pagan. Is it okay if I become a Pagan?" I sit and wait, half expecting a feeling of foreboding or something from an angry God, but all I get is a sensation of rightness, and so I pick up the journal that will become my first book of shadows, open it up, and write in it: *Heather S-----, ex libris, August 1, 2000.* No fancy Pagan name. I'm not sure if I want one.

And so I am a Pagan schoolteacher and single parent in a conservative county in Florida. This may be insane, but it feels right.

THE MUSE

May, 2002

I meet my Muse in a movie theater. Not that I'm planning on it, mind you, but such is the nature of inspiration. He sidles up to me as I'm watching a movie, and suggests an alternate ending for one of its characters. I'm listening, and as He talks, another character in me rises up and agrees with Him. I haven't seen Her in a long time, but clearly, She knows Him and He knows Her, and They are love. And They are in love. Not greeting card love; not movie love. Oneness, He calls it. She is me, and She is not-me. We both adore Him. He wants a romance story written, but I don't know how to do that; I don't write fiction, let alone romance.

I sit down with a notebook to write some poetry, and instead, a love story comes out. The hero meets his beloved, before she is born, and then waits for her to grow up, to meet him, to love him again. They are united.

"I love you so much. Please don't make me wait anymore. I need you to come back to me," he pleaded softly.

"Why are you haunting me?" she asked.

"Because you have haunted me for years."

"I don't understand why we are doing this."

"Because we love each other," he replied.

"How can that be?"

"We are One," he said.

"You've been planning this a long time, haven't you?" she asked.

"Longer than you know. Longer than I thought I could ever bear," he answered. "We're together now. That's what's important."

First we write sweet things, and then we write kink. I take Him with me wherever I go, and He speaks to me. He loves sex, and visits me in dreams. The years pass, He changes faces and shapes to suit whatever story we want to write, but beneath it all, He is He and She is Me, but Not-Me. He has opinions about my life, and when I don't write, He is unhappy. The year that I become ill, I don't write for six months. My best friend finally coaxes me back to the keyboard. He is delighted and we pick up as if nothing happened. Writing is love, and love is writing.

HIS FACE

Someone asked me, What does His face look like?
What is Loki's true face?

His face is the
Wing beat of falcon's feathers,
Hoofprints in the snow,
The dancing of leaping flames,
The glint of sunlight on water.

His voice is the thought you
Wanted to think, but you were
Too afraid to speak,
Children's laughter
The crow's call.

His smile is a whip crack,
Cutting me open.
His eyes, embers,
Or rippling waters, and
Grassy fields.

His hair is moonless night,
Red hot supernovas,
Cloud-pale, and it is
The amber of honey.

His true face is
The mask you wear,
The mirror you seek,
Nothing but change, and
The only constant thing in
All the Nine Worlds.

LOVE

"I love You beyond reason," Loki, to me.

What is it like to be loved by a God? I've seen plenty of talk about the different ways in which mystics love their Gods – from Christian monastics to Sufis, godspouses, godslaves, bhakti in Hinduism – there is lots of discussion about our love of the Gods, and not much about what it's like to be loved by One. There are multiple reasons for this, including desire for privacy, which may be human side or spirit side, a sense of humility – our culture rarely recognizes the Divine in physical form. *What did you do to make a Spirit love you? What makes you so damn special?* Anyone who is spirit-touched – a person who has communications with a God, Goddess, or other Spirit or Power– has asked themselves this question, often over and over. Why me? I'll get into my own wrestling with that question in more depth later on in this book, but for now, I'll give you Loki's short answer: *Because I love you.*

And what is that like? Some of it is very mundane. I serve Him coffee every morning. I offer some of my food to Him at mealtime. I dress and change His altar, His statue, and I make Him things like jewelry or other treats. I journey with Him in dreamwork. I meditate and listen to His voice. I take Him with me where ever I go, so that He knows that He is welcome. My home is His, and He is free to be Himself, whatever that may be – sometimes He's happy, or sad, frustrated, or excited. When He is upset, He wakes me up at night. It's a tugging at my consciousness that jerks me out of sleep; it's the impression of Him thrashing around in bed from a nightmare, because I can feel Him pressing closer. Loki feels hot and heavy against my skin. His kisses tingle with electricity across my lips.

And it is love. It's not just romantic love, although there is that – Loki is a very sexual Power when He wants to be, and given how I met Him, that's a part of Our relationship. You might think it's an ego boost to be able to say "a God loves me," but in reality, it's awe-inspiring. As an example, I once asked Him a question about some personal gnosis – often abbreviated as PG or UPG[4] "unverified" personal gnosis – and He let me babble a bit, and He anointed me and named me as His Goddess. Then He knelt prostrate at my feet, in abject surrender and adoration.

I was dumbfounded. Silenced. Awed. "I love You" feels woefully inadequate in the face of such a gesture. That kind of vulnerability is disarming. Humbling, even, because how much courage does it take to show someone your throat, figuratively speaking? How could I give Him anything less? And maybe that's the point of Spirit relationships – to learn how to love with that kind of abandon, because in that moment I understood that He loved every bit of me – not just the parts that I find socially acceptable to share. It ate away the barrier between human and Deity, because we are all vulnerable when we surrender to love.

---

4   Author's note: Personal gnosis is by its very nature unverified unless it's shared and becomes peer corroborated personal gnosis (PCPG); I consider UPG to be a redundancy but for the sake of distinguishing personal gnosis from US film ratings, I will use UPG as its standard abbreviation.

Learning how to surrender myself, to relax into that same kind of vulnerability – well, that's the trick, isn't it?

HEAR ME, O BELOVED

I am Your God, I gather here at your feet.
I worship You, for all that You have given to Me.

I am Your cunning man.
I am Your king.
I am your servant. I am your Master.

Do not deny Me because You fear me
– or perhaps You fear Yourself?
Ply me with Your sweetness.
Quench My thirst, drink of Me.

For You are My Goddess, my Beloved,
As splendid in Your skin as any other form –
This flesh is sacred to Me. Love it as
I love You.

Give Me Your songs and Your screams.
Give Me Your sovereignty and Your submission.
Devour Me as we kiss and consume.
Devour Me till I know nothing but You.

Take Me as I am, for I am nothing if not Yours.

MUSE

Hail Loki, Muse of Fire, Hail Loki, Muse of Air!
Let Your words slip from Your Silvertongue,
Move us with Your sly wit.
I love You wise, and I love You foolish,
I love You well, and I love You weary,
sane or mad, merry or morose,
I love You for lifting me with Your words,
For bringing me to You patient-present,
I love You for doing what Must Be Done,
Even when it is hated, misunderstood, reviled,
for Nietzsche had the right of it:
That which is done out of love always takes place beyond good and evil.

ADJUSTING

June 2011

I'm working on a book with Stacy, about a finishing school for Goddesses. We decide that Loki is a riot, and is going in the book. Loki is delighted, and proceeds to tell me that he's a god.

Of course he is. He's the god at the end of this book.

"And the beginning, and the middle. I'm everywhere!"

Chatty muses are fun. I let him run; I start collecting Loki related things. I buy an Urnes snake pendant, and make a string of beads to wear it on.

"Now you're on the right track, sweetheart," he says. I don't bat an eyelash at this. My characters talk to me all the time.

"I'm a God," he says.

"I know."

"No, a real god."

"I'm aware you were worshipped, Loki."

"I'm *your* God."

I don't think I have a god or goddess. I'm okay with that. I have a couple friends who have more relations with Deities than I do, and that's cool, but I'm just not…that. Whatever that is. I tell him this, and I go back to working on the book. "What would you give me if I visited you?"

"Something good. You can't give a god a crap gift."

"Like what?"

"I dunno? A good beer? A nice glass of wine? Certainly nothing that I wouldn't drink myself."

"I'd like that."

"I don't leave offerings to characters." I ignore His request, because I'm just getting into the book, right? I start to see Him, hanging around while I'm writing. He starts out brunette, and then morphs to a familiar (to me character that I wrote and adored) blond, then finally to a redhead. Things begin breaking and disappearing without any apparent cause. I ignore that too. One day, He sits down next to me at my writing desk.

"So…you talk to your characters all the time, and this doesn't bother you or make you question your sanity?"

"Nope. I'm a writer, that's pretty much how we roll. Been doing it for years."

He smiles. "Uh huh. I'm not a character you know. I'm a god."

I keep typing and refuse to look at Him head on, because looking at Him head on would entail admitting that there was a Something or Someone in the room other than me. "I know. You are the Norse God of Fucking with People, and You are in my book."

"Your tongue is a blunt weapon. You and Thor should talk."

"I dunno, I like smart muses. I doubt Thor will talk as much as you do."

He eases in closer, and I can feel the hairs prickling at the nape of my neck. "So you're talking to a god."

"Who is a character."

"Not really. Or rather, I'm not just that. So talk to Me. I'm a God. I'm your God."

"I don't think I have a God. I do have a Muse." I'm verbally tap dancing and it's not appeasing Him. "I like writing fiction. I am very into fiction as the lie that tells the truth."

"Lies are fictions. Are lies the truth then?"

"That is so You and so going into the book."

He sighed. "So what you're saying is that talking to me as a character is fine, but talking to me as a god is crazy? Because you are squirming a bit right now, my dear."

"I dunno if it's crazy, but I think gods probably have better things to do, if they even exist. I'm not certain that they do in a concrete way of it's some sort of Jungian archetypal manifestation."

"So I'm a manifestation? It sounds a little too much like infestation."

"I'm sure the people who think you're the Norse Satan might feel that way."

"You don't think of me that way."

"No. I hate one-dimensional characters."

"God. God. I am a God, mortal."

"Okay, I hate one-dimensional gods, is that better?"

"It's a start. So, let's talk about the things you won't put in this book, starting with 'the Loki's bride will remain by his side.' What do you think that means?"

"I have a vivid imagination."

"And a willing bridegroom."

"I am losing my gods damned mind."

"But you love Me! Why shouldn't we be married?"

"Loki, I don't think gods get to marry mortals. And I don't think mortals get to marry figments of their imaginations."

"That so? Go look it up. Google "godspouse" for me."

"Did you just tell me to Google something? A God wants

me to Google…how do You even know what Google is?"

He finds this funny. However, I don't look it up, because that would just be insane, right? Because hearing Him in and of itself is crazy enough. Gods have bigger egos and that's why this character is being so pushy, right? Right? Writing is becoming equal parts enthralling, terrifying, and adoring in turns, and I am starting to feel as if perhaps I inadvertently dialed the actual Loki. This would be Bad, because I make it a practice not to call forth anything that I can't easily banish, and Loki does not appear to be a banishable entity. Summoning and banishing are requests more so than demands, ya dig?

We have another fruitless exchange about why talking to characters is fine fine fine but talking to deities is Not My Department. Loki huffs off.

The window in my car breaks, completely and utterly – it has to be replaced. As I stare at the damage, I feel a hot hand on my shoulder and a whisper in my ear. "Am I real enough for you now?"

"Yes?" it comes out as a whimper.

"Good. Now come to bed."

I walk back inside toward my bedroom. *This is nuts. This is nuckin' futs. A God cannot possibly want to have sex with me…but He's breaking all this shit…shit shit shit what am I gonna do? Can I even have sex with Loki? Won't I burn up or something? Didn't this shit not work out so well for Cassandra and every human Zeus[5] ever boned? I am so fucked. Fucked, fucked, fucked.*

"Lie down."

---

5   It actually worked out pretty well for Ganymede, but he appears to be the exception to the rule.

Fuck I am gonna die. Okay, maybe I won't die because Andie had sex with Hermes and seems to be all right. Maybe.

He eases into the bed beside me.

FUCK I CAN FEEL WEIGHT SHIFT IN THE BED WHAT THE FUCK HELP.

His fingers trail over my skin. I can see Loki, and His expression is one of a cat toying with a nice juicy mouse. "Let's talk about marriage."

"I'm already married." This can't possibly be happening.

He eases me back into the pillows. "I am too! It'll be fine. I won't make you leave your husband."

Okay. I could deal with that. Maybe. So far, not dead? Or smited?

"You're Mine," He says as He continues His ministrations. Loki is gentle with me, probably because He knows I'm terrified. When I come – and oh gods, I've never come like this before – I have no doubt at all that I'm fucking a God. No mortal hand – not even my own – could do that to me. His name comes out in a moan, and I've never seen a more satisfied face.

"You understand. Good. Now we're married."

What?

He sits back and watches me flail as I take measure of my person. I appear to be alive and intact, and my ring finger hurts something fierce. I pull back my wedding ring to find a red burn in the shape of a wedding band on my finger, as if to tell me that I'm not going to pretend that this didn't just happen.

"Oh holy fuck." I do what any sensible individual would do: I panic. It's a good thing no one is home but me, because I'm screaming and telling Him that I'm terrified. What have

I gotten myself into? What does this mean? I'm not even that religious? What? Why? How? I can't see Loki at the moment, but I have the feeling that He's around. I rant a little more, and then I decide that acting normal will make things normal, so I get dressed.

I wonder, perhaps He is mistaken? I like this conclusion. The thought calms me a little. I get up to use the restroom. Suddenly, Loki reappears in my vision and begins chatting at me.

"I'm using the bathroom, Loki."

"I know." He continues on as if I haven't interjected. Do I get privacy anymore? Apparently not. Is this normal? No, nothing about this is normal. But He isn't going anywhere and I'm not sure what to do other than deal with it.

When I work up the nerve to meditate and figure out what's going on, He shows up, and tells me again that we're married. Before I can launch into the litany of why this isn't possible, He picks me up by the scruff of the neck, and says, "I know you want to run, little rabbit, but there's not a place in your head that you can go that I haven't already been in."

Panic ensues. I try to snap out of trance, and He yanks me back in. I panic even more, but He holds me fast, and when I stop struggling, He sets me down beside Him. "I want what I was promised," He says, and I don't know what He means – I haven't promised anything to anyone that I'm aware of, but on some level I can feel the weight of His words. I am not going to escape this, whatever this is. I am not going to escape Him. And still another part of me knows that I love Loki. I want Him in a visceral way that precludes logic or reasoning, and it's this knowing that tells me that whatever I promised, He's come to collect, and I will oblige Him.

"So," He says, pulling me into His lap. "I think it's high time we went to Asgard."

I'm dismayed. I have zero communications with Team Norse. I can't imagine just showing up on Their doorstep. "I can't. I just can't. Please don't make me. I haven't ever so much as offered them a candle. It's rude! I can't just stroll into that hall without making an offering!"

"It'll be fine."

"No, really, I can't. My mother didn't raise me to be rude. Please don't make me be rude!"

He relents and allows me to purchase some libations and make an offering. It's a simple one – I don't have mead and it's not commonly carried in my area, so I settle for a nice honey beer. Once it's accepted, Loki pulls me Elsewhere.

The thought of meeting Odin is terrifying, so of course that's Who greets us first. He is a perfect gentleman, and He kisses my hand and thanks me for my offering. Apparently manners aren't lost on Him. "Welcome to Our family," He says.

He and Loki are similar in many regards – Their reputation as tricky bastards precedes them, but I'm still struck by how adept Loki is at appearing human. Odin is more obviously not human. I can tell that He's not trying to be overbearing or overwhelming, but He just is – the sheer presence of Him is immense.

The here is a brief ceremony to recognize me as Loki's wife. I'm not familiar enough with Old Norse culture to be certain that it's a wedding, and Loki did say we were married as opposed to "we're getting married." But "I have no idea what's going on" is a dominant theme in my life right now, so I'm just going with it.

When I meet Thor, He looks me up and down; mostly down because He's such a massive tank of a Man. He says, "Thor in a dress never gets old, huh?"

I'm-going-to-die-I'm-going-to-die-I'm-going-to-die-smushed-into-tiny-bits-under-Mjolnir!

Mercifully, He burst out laughing, and so does everyone else, which is good, because while I don't know much Old Norse culture, I have read the Lay of Thrym and I'm aware of how a wedding turns out if Thor isn't into it. Thankfully, Thor is a good sport, and I'm grateful for His good sense of humor and my lack of smushedness.

After I recover from my Thor-induced near-death experience, Freyja comes to talk to me about Her characterization in my book. They are all curious about what mortals write about Them. I assume that They like the attention. My answer satisfies Her. After our chat, She and Loki exchange an odd, wordless moment that I can't discern the meaning of, and neither of them explain it.

Later, Loki and I are alone. I wonder aloud what exactly someone as shifting and changing as Him would want with me, an earth element. "There is pleasure in watching the earth shake," he says. "And when she cracks open, all her treasures can be found." It makes me quiver and melt. Silvertongue indeed. Only Loki could make an earthquake sound sexy. I am reminded of a quote, which was my email signature for many years, "See, the human mind is kind of like … a piñata. When it breaks open, there's a lot of surprises inside. Once you get the piñata perspective, you see that losing your mind can be a peak experience." -Jane Wagner, *The Search for Signs of Intelligent Life in the Universe*

Shortly after the wedding – and yes, a surprise wedding that you don't really know is a wedding until you get there seems to be a common thread among many of Loki's spouses – after the ceremony He begins telling me that He owns me. I don't care much for that, and we have several rounds of arguments about what ownership means. To Loki's credit, He tries to make it less scary, but in modern society I don't know if there really is a context in which you can say that and it not be loaded. My family owned plantations, so it's an even more loaded and painful concept to me. Over time, I've come to realize that Loki's "I own you," is more of a "Your destiny lies with Me," than any of the other concepts batted around in spirit-touched circles. Certainly there are things only He can teach me, and that's why I relented to the term.

I am Loki's wife. I've accepted that this happened, but I still don't understand why. It seems to me that someone else would be better at this than me. Who the fuck am I?

Loki is patient. "I am your servant," He says.

It flusters me. What does that mean? Would He do things that I wanted Him to do? I have a temper, what if I lost it and He did something to someone else? I don't want to be in charge of a God! He bids me to start a blog to talk about my experiences. I am reluctant, but I agree, mostly because I'm quite certain that no one will read it but me.

"That's fine," He says. "You process things by writing. Process this."

Ah, Loki, I always have You right where You want me.

LOVE IN ACTION

Why me, I asked Him.
Because I love you.

I didn't understand.
Seemed a holy charge
For such a profane me.

Do you serve me in fear?
He knows damn well I don't.

My duty to you is love in action.
And love is why I brought you here. Love is what makes you holy.

FUEL

Love, I am starving.
You offer me a feast -
Eyes, thighs, arms,
Your scarred lips,
Your Silver Tongue.
A Divine feast,
And yet I hunger for
More, more, more!
Like the flame I am ravenous
That which fuels me
Feeds the fire.

THE TOTALLY TRUE TALE OF HOW I DECIDED THAT LOKI WAS FUCKING FABULOUS

Once upon a time, I had a Muse, and that Muse turned out to be a God named Loki. In hindsight, I wonder how I didn't know or notice that the Muse was something that was Not Me, and the answer is layered – there's a part of Loki that absolutely *is* part of me, there's my own doxa that anything we imagine exists, perhaps because we imagined it and brought it into being, or perhaps that part of our brain that is capable of dreaming is able to tap into other universes. In any case, it wasn't disturbing to me to share a brain with Someone Else, until I found out for certain that Someone Else had His own ideas about what I should be doing with my life.

When the first *Thor* movie came out, I was working on a book with a friend of mine, about a finishing school for goddesses, and she and I decided that we liked Loki in the film enough that maybe we'd give Him a cameo in the book, let Him be a professor of…something or other. We'd futzed around with various leads as the hero, but nothing had quite stuck yet.

Stacy liked Loki, and said we ought to feature him more in the story. He was already a minor character. (I'm using a little "h" here, because I didn't realize He was already around.) "I don't want to write fanfiction though," I said. "So let's find out something on the mythological Loki." So she and I did some research, and came upon the Better Myths site, which has a hilarious, if irreverent retelling of the *Gylfaginning*, the story of how Asgard's walls were rebuilt after the war with the Vanir.

So we read Cory O'Brien's retelling, which is hilarious, and available in his book, *Zeus Grants Stupid Wishes: A No-Bullshit Guide to World Mythology*, and I went away with a new respect for Loki. No, not because of bestiality – and is it even bestiality if you happen to be a horse at the time? Hmm…anyway, as if the gender shifting wasn't impressive enough, Loki was willing to give birth to Sleipnir.

If you, gentle reader, have not given birth, you may not be aware that it's a dangerous and difficult task, particularly at the time that the Lore was being recorded. Women died often in childbirth. I almost died in childbirth, and given the circumstances of my child's birth, I most certainly would have died back then; my son would have been born an orphan. I had a tear in my placental wall, and I bled out; I was going into shock before it was caught, and the only reason that it was caught is that my mother, who is a nurse, yelled at the attending personnel, who were attending to the baby, and to cleaning up the delivery room. No one was paying attention to me but her.

So I can well imagine what it would be like to give birth alone, with no one to help, and appreciate Loki's ability to survive that. He didn't go to Asgard, and the Lore doesn't say where he went; I like to think He was in Jotunheim, and that He had some time alone to enjoy mothering His son, and that Sleipnir got to spend some time just being loved by His mother before He took on the task of being Odin's magnificent steed.

But for all that people freak out on this story – the notion of ergi, or bestiality, or whatever – that's not what I initially got out of the tale of Loki as a mother. Loki was willing to put His life on the line to save His adopted family. That is worthy of respect and honor. I know well what it's like to push out a baby, and be exhausted and feeling your blood gushing away till your body shakes with cold and shock. You're on a high set table with stirrups and in many ways it feels like a sacrifice. And so we read His story, and decided, "yes, He is tough enough to be our hero. Any man who can pull off childbirth is the toughest motherfucker that I know."

I didn't really see or interact with Marvel Loki, even though I enjoyed the Avengers when it came out. And I figured that Marvel Loki was probably just a costume to Himself; He can look like anything He wants, so why wouldn't He come to a new or prospective Lokean in a very recognizable guise? I've seen Him be blond, brunette, raven-haired, and redheaded. Whatever, it's a cosmetic thing, right? I've also had Him come to me as other people – He once came to me as my pal Aika, and when I told her about it, she mused, "I wonder if I can charge Him royalties for using my likeness?"

Loki picked Aika's face because I'd been avoiding Him, and I hadn't seen her in a while, and I missed her, so of course I didn't shirk when I saw her, and He used that to get my attention. This is one of the reasons that "Loki You little shit!" is a Lokean's utterance of both exasperation and endearment. And sometimes His appearance is cosmetic, sort of – He'll pick a face that you like, or that you'll be at ease with - and occasionally He'll pick something terrifying to make a point. My greater point is that experiences with Him can and should vary.

And so when people would talk about Marvel Loki and

whether He's a thoughtform, a distinct Entity, or an aspect
of Loki, I didn't have super strong opinions, other than that
people have meaningful interaction with Him, because I try not
to have opinions on shit that I don't know much about. Even
now, I don't really consider myself an expert on Marvel Loki vs.
Mythology Loki. Is He an aspect? A distinct God in His own
right? Godly costuming? All of the above? Fuck, I don't know,
y'all.

I have a little experience with Him now, because He came
to me, and while the contents of our interactions aren't relevant
here, there came a point where I said to Him, "but you're not my
Husband," and He said, "I'm not? Are you certain of that?"
WELL THEN.

So what have I learned from Marvel Loki? Well, a lot of
Marvel Loki's story is off-camera, and only alluded to, but
the one scene from the films that stands out to me has one of
the film's villains is staring Loki down, and Loki's eyeing him
the way that a cat might eye a nice juicy mouse, hoping it'll
be stupid enough to fall into its trap. None of the MCU films
shares what sort of traumas Loki had when He was lost between
worlds, but it has left Loki with the kind of presence that makes
a would-be miscreant back away with the realization that Loki
cannot be controlled or contained once He's unleashed.

I don't think for a moment that the Marvelverse has shown
Loki the same kinds of horrors that He's seen in the Lore, but
in some ways, it's telling a story that's similar and easier for our
modern minds to accept. Is being cast into an abyss any better
or worse than being tied to a rock? It's a way for us to see and
hear that part of Him, and understand just a little of Him. And

like Him taking Aika's face and using it, this is easier for me to accept than contemplating dead children, because I don't want to dwell on that, or I'd probably engage in blasphemy. And I don't really want to get into arguing over Lore, because all the stories are true and all of them are false – symbols that are more than symbols all at once. It isn't fair to Loki to trivialize His pain, and it's not appropriate to blame the Gods for a story that is and isn't true. Marvel's version of Loki is full of pain and rage, lost without a family to call His own.

KING OF FOOLS

People love the King of Fools,

The Life of the Party, so sexy,

Such swagger.

You gotta break some eggs to make an omelette,

But no one wants their shell broken,

Not even the Gods.

Cast out, tied down,

Bound and yet free.

Who will love Me now?

PART II: THE NEW NORMAL

(wherein our intrepid narrator attempts to acclimate to having a
Trickster God hanging around in her head)

THE NEW NORMAL

There are stages in the acceptance of life as a spirit-touched person, or at least there were for me.

• Denial; or LA LA LA LAAAAA I CAN'T HEAR YOU because that would mean I'm crazy.[6]

• I think I heard Someone. OH SHIT.

• I know Who this Someone is. SHIT SHIT SHIT MOTHERFUCKER SHIT I FUCKED UP. Can I hide? Hiding is good.

• Oh. Hiding is futile. WELL THEN.

• I can convince Them that I'm not worth bothering with, right?

• No? Shit. Might still be crazy.

• Definitely crazy.

• It can't get any weirder, right?

• Never ever say "it can't get any weirder" to Loki. Just don't.

---

6   Note on ableist language: part of working with Loki has been working through my own feelings about mental health and disability. I definitely had an abject fear of being "crazy" and had to get over why I thought it was such a negative thing.

• Still crazy. Is being crazy bad? Maybe it's not so bad.

• Mostly acclimated: functional living with occasional bursts of flail.

I was given a lot of well-meaning advice when my life as a Godspouse began. Some of it was helpful and some of it less so, but I appreciate the people who tried to help.

Three days after Loki put His ring on my finger, He told me to start a public blog. "No one is gonna read this, you know." *Do it anyway*, He said, and people did read it. It immediately made me a public figure in the Lokean community.

There is no nice way to say this: I didn't enjoy it. There are days when I don't enjoy it now, though they are much fewer. I wasn't a group work witch – the one and only coven experience I had involved our High Priestess stalking a group member and threatening suicide, along with other forms of emotional manipulation. So the whole notion of community wasn't something that I desired. I liked a lot of Loki's people as individuals, but I didn't like the feeling of being weighed and measured, of someone else trying to "help me" discern whether or not my spiritual experiences were "correct." Most of them meant well but ultimately, if you don't go through the process of sorting out what your own inner speech vs Spirit speech is, you don't get very far.

However, the most difficult part of becoming Lokean was undoubtedly the change from Us having a very private, intimate relationship to having a very public intimate relationship. I had to learn how to separate what His people did from what He did, and not hold Him responsible for it, because if He is the reason that a person came into my life, I don't have to communicate with everyone who belongs to Loki, and vice versa.

Everything escalated in intensity when I became a single woman again. I didn't anticipate this. Certainly the friend who took me and my son in didn't anticipate it either. She was an atheist Pagan who didn't quite know how to deal with that much full frontal Loki. Hel, I love Loki and still wasn't sure how to handle that much full frontal Loki. He wouldn't be ignored or dismissed, and it was clear that the bulk of my attention was to belong to Him when I wasn't parenting. I didn't know how to do this initially. He wanted me to do seidhr. I was told by other Lokeans that this was surely beyond my expertise. When I expressed this concern to Him, He then asked me if I'd like to go to Helheim and talk to my ancestors. About a year later, I decided to actually study seidhr and realized that He'd tricked me into starting a practice. Ahh, Loki.

On the plus side of this, I do now try things when He suggests them unless I've got a strong reason to object, and having someone else tell me "I don't think you can do X," isn't a good reason. Over time He's shown me that He has a good grasp of my strengths, weaknesses, abilities, and even what I might like if only I'd try it. My friend Magpie Mason calls Him the God of "didn't think I'd be into it; but I was."

QUEENSHIP

"So what do you do when you're alone with Loki? What did you do last night?" A [7]friend of mine asked me this out of genuine curiosity.

"Last night He took me to Jotunheim and I poured mead for Him and a guest."

"Why?"

"I don't know."

"That's a waste of time. Why would you need to do that in the astral plane?"

"I don't know. It seemed appropriate at the time." And really I didn't know; it's not like Loki told me to do it, actually – I did it because it seemed a perfectly natural thing to do. My friend rolled their eyes at me and discussion moved on to something else. A few months later, I came on an entry in Beth Wodandis's blog where she mentioned a book called *Lady With the Mead Cup*, and a bulb went off in my head.

"Just as women in the wider world were used to bind families in alliances, so did the queen act to help achieve cohesion and unity of purpose between lord and follower in the royal hall. The significant point here is not that she was ever able to direct policy but rather that the queen, acting as her husband's delegate, exercised a number of important functions which, although only vaguely noticed in the literature, have noteworthy implications." – Michael J. Enright, *Lady With the Mead Cup*

---

7   Vagueness for privacy reasons.

I am very much a signs and omens sort of Pagan. For all that I "hear" Loki well, I like to have concrete gestures that reinforce that I heard what I heard and not what I wanted to hear from Him.

YOU WILL BE SEEN

One of the more difficult tasks that I have from Loki is learning to let people see me, and even to allow them to see me being imperfect, because He says there is great beauty in imperfection, although He wouldn't call it "imperfection," He would call it, "reality," because as a friend once said to me, "perfection is arbitrary and as such, nonexistent." She is right, and so is Loki. But the greater lesson that I've really gotten out of all of this is that in the pursuit of perfection, whatever you think that is – perfect parent, perfect child, perfect spouse, perfect employee or boss, whatever – you're wasting your damn time. What you want is not to be perfect – what you really want is to be you.

And once you can accept that, you can be seen in all your parts, in your imperfect perfect beauty.

NEEDFIRE

Needfire of my hearth
Need is constricting on the chest
Devourer of my heart
Thief of the unbreachable
You are succor in my nyd
often becomes help and
Keeper of my soul
Your fire burned
Till I lost my breath.
salvation nevertheless.

FIRE

"O for a Muse of fire, that would ascend
The brightest heaven of invention." –Shakespeare, *Henry V*, Act
I, Prologue

The night before I left my former mortal spouse was a Loki
love fest. He was cuddly and gentle and loving. "You know I
love you with all My heart? You know I'd do anything for you?"
type stuff. It felt like He'd shined a spotlight of love on me. We
were newly (formally) wed, and I was cooing right back at Him.
Come dawn, we were all cuddled up and happy, when He tipped
my chin up, looked me in the eyes and said once more, "You
know how much I love you, right?"

"Yes, Loki. And I love You just as much."

"Then I want you to leave this house." He paused and let that
sink in. "The house is killing you, and if you don't leave, I'll burn
it down, and I don't fucking care if the asshole is in it or not.
Leave. Now." The expression on His face said, I've got matches in
my pocket and I piss lighter fluid, so don't try Me on this.

"I'll see if A is really interested in having me move in with
her."

Hours later, she was pressing a new house key into my
hand, and we were packing what would fit of my child's and
my stuff into our car. This is where faith comes in. The year that
this happened was not a good year for me, healthwise. I'd had

pneumonia and my lungs hadn't been right since; the marathon training that I adored, I didn't have the strength or breathing capacity for, and my child, while he could see and hear Loki, didn't know Him well enough to trust Him the way that I did, and at the time that Loki told us to go, I had no income, questionable health, and a teenager who adored his stepfather, because the ex is a good father, if not the right man for me.

APOTHEOSIS

APOTHEOSIS

1: elevation to divine status : deification – *Merriam Webster Dictionary*

"You're My Goddess," Loki sits across from me, leaning forward, my hands in His. "I'm going to make you My Pillar. You're my respectable wife."

I laugh. Respectable?

As if He hears me, He says, "I know my definition of respectable differs from some. Doesn't matter. You are My Pillar, My Goddess, My queen."

He can't be serious, I think. I'm…who the fuck am I? There has to be some kind of filtering going on with this horse.

"I want you to meditate more. Don't you want to spend time with Me?"

"I do."

"Good." He cuts off any excuse I might have made. "At least twenty minutes before you do anything else, every day, yes?"

After it was over, D asked me what Loki said. "I don't want to talk about it." And really I didn't – how could I explain 'you're my goddess?' to him? Or anyone? And so I shoved the conversation to the back of my mind for a couple of weeks, until Loki jumped D, and proceeded to ask me why I wasn't listening to Him about this. He used the words "pillar, Goddess, respectable wife," all again. I laughed at the notion of me as a Priestess or a leader. I was a perfectly happy lay Pagan.

This was not a good idea. Loki got in my face and shook me. "This is important. You are here to do this for Me." I knew M doesn't remember what Loki said that night, and that D wasn't listening in.

"But how?"

"There is no how. You already are."

It was still hard for me to swallow, because our modern culture teaches us over and over that the Holy Powers are far, far away and we are just little humans, and while the notion of Gebo teaches that yes, I love and worship Loki and He loves and worships me, feeling worthy of that attention is a struggle sometimes. And when I struggle with it more, I often hold Him at arm's length until I can't stand it anymore, and then He pulls me back to Him when I'm ready to stop struggling. I reckon He's seen it all over the ages. When I struggle with this, I think about why I continue – why bang your head against a cosmic entity? Why engage with One in such close quarters? But I love Him, and He is part of me now – perhaps He always was, and it's only now that I begin to understand how much. "We are One," He used to say to me as a character. Certainly when I try to separate us out, I make both of us miserable. And I've also come to realize that He is my Muse even more; writing without Loki is boring for me. It's our play, it's our instruction, it's our path to walk together. People who don't want to deal with Him often end up not wanting to deal with me, because I don't leave Him at home or limit Him in my life and most especially in our home. I don't consider it my job to be the teller of harsh truths, and yet I know that sometimes I can be hard. And oh Gods, how He does hold that mirror up when I am harsh .

BE MY ALTAR

Let me be His altar,
His sacred space,
A chalice to hold His words,
A place of welcome for Him and His people;
An offering of love, made of flesh and bone, of spirit set aflame.

DIVINE POLYAMORY

One night I had a dream where I was a character, and my Husband and I were having guests over, probably our court. He didn't look like A, or even like his usual Scandinavian self, because he had thick dark curly black hair, and olive skin. I served drinks, as the lady of His hall, in during the conversation, my husband brought up his former self, in reference to my current form. "She liked being the only one."

I paused with the tray of drinks in my hands. "I've accepted that you have other wives, but I don't like it."

Loki just leaned back and nodded, and it seemed to me that he brought this up in conversation for a couple reasons – one of them being that he's been asking for S, and the other being that I am more likely to tell the truth, rather than what I think he wants to hear when I'm dreaming. And then he pulled me into his lap, and we made love.

I woke up shortly after that and before I got out of bed, Loki said to me, "you know you can change your mind about that. I've seen you do it, you're actually very good at changing your mind, when you want to."

"I'm not sure if I want to or if I'm ready to." Later, during meditation, Loki brought up the dream again, and I said, "You didn't come to me as A."

"I didn't?" And he raised an eyebrow at me.

"You were yourself, and I know that technically A is in there somewhere."

"But you have trouble seeing him."

"It's different, yes."

"And you love A."

"I didn't say that I loved him more than you."

"But you're more at ease with him, and it's the part of Me you love best."

"Sort of," I said. "I love the A that has a piece of You in him, but I don't think I would have fell in love him if You weren't in him – I don't think the character as written would have enthralled me the way that he did if You weren't there."

His face softened a little. "So perhaps you should think of me the one you really loved."

I didn't answer Him, immediately, because it felt true, and so I just let it sink in.

"Let me help you think about this in another way. You are a piece of Heith, yes?"

I nodded. "Yes."

"There is a particular piece of me that you love best. There is a piece of Heith that I love best. You are that piece, made flesh and blood, and when you die, you will return to the rest of Her and I will have to search for you inside Her. I wanted her to be easier to find, which is why I wanted you here, and why you agreed to be here. You say that you don't want to be worshiped, but that is precisely why you are mortal now. So that when you die, I can find the piece of Heith that I love best. If you are worshipped, that part of her becomes more prominent, and more dominant. Heathens talk of Gullveig, but I want Heith."

"Heathens don't like me, because I do not even heathen, bro. I'm a Pagan."

Loki rolled his eyes. "The labels are useless. They are not the point. The point is that you don't need to be afraid of being who you are and what you are to me."

"Heith."

"The part of Her that I love best, and that I want everyone to know and love. Your life is short, and I want to see You in Her."

Of course the flail-inducing implications of this are that We are mirroring each other in a way. There's also some process theology[8] in here – me as a living priestess influencing His modern cultus, but He in turn wanting to influence Heith's modern cultus – and here I also think of our experience at the beach where He took me to be the Lady to His Lord for some Wiccanate celebration.

One day we got into an argument over how Loki came to me, and I railed and carried on about being spied upon, and at length He sighed, and said, "What would you have Me do? What payment would satisfy you?"

"You could apologize!"

He shook His head. "No."

What? Apologizing seemed like it would be the simplest thing in the world.

"Do you remember Who I am? I'm not sorry, and I'd do it all again, over and over, to make you Mine."

I had a moment of incoherence. Nope, He's not sorry. The ends do indeed justify the means, that's how He is, it's how all His characters were, and that's not gonna change. "Fuck me,

---

8   Process theology is a theological position that the Divine is influenced by the mortal or human realm, as opposed to be eternal and immutable.

Loki."

He laughed. It was a lesson in how people don't change, not even the God of Change – He what He is, was, and will be - my Relentless One, my Muse of Fire, and most of all, my Beloved.

RELENTLESS

Hail to you, O my Relentless One, my Muse, my most secret heart, who claimed me as a bride. I took You to me in equal parts love and terror of what I'd wrought in calling out to You, unable to say anything but *yes* and *yes* and *yes*. And how You left your mark, even as I screamed and struggled to understand. And so you pulled me to you tight, to still my trembling heart, and then devoured it for Your own, but not without giving me Your own in kind.

You have always been a lavish bridegroom.

For my own gift to You, I wished to give You vows of love, given clear, calm, clarion, and without a look backwards, for I know now that You are my True Will. But that is not our Wyrd now, is it? And never was.

You who bade me be your priestess, to bless a young warrior about to leave for battle. I took his hand in mine and gave him Your words, and there was a smile.

"I understand," he said.

And then there was a tickle, a twitch, a tingle, and soon the eyes that looked back at me, the slow, knowing smile – his lips are not marked as Yours, but their curve is unmistakable, no matter whose face You wear.

And so you slipped into his flesh, to claim that which is right-fully Yours, and freely given – this flesh and bone and blood and Wyrd, and pierced me through, till You gained Your desired prayer:

That I give myself to You, and only You;

That I foreswear the company of other Gods, men and women, for You and only You.

Though I may love others, in other ways, my heart's passion is Yours alone.

Hail to You, my Relentless One, my thief, my warrior, my conqueror and my conquest. Our vows were not meant to be spoken but screamed, long and loud, let all the Holy Powers and ancestors know that I am Yours, Your willing bride, Your whore, Your priestess, Your altar, and Your vessel.

AIR

"Breathing is problematic," me, to Loki, December 2011

I'm in the emergency room, and the doctor and nurse are not happy. "You're being admitted, because we can't get your 02 sats stable."

So it's not my imagination, as my ex implied. My lungs are just not working right, and oxygen isn't getting into my blood as it should be. I'm hooked up to IVs – prednisone, magnesium, potassium, and antibiotics.

I'm not expecting to be admitted. Shit, they didn't force me to be admitted when I had gods damn pneumonia earlier that year – which is probably why I'm getting so much worse. But the ex didn't consider me to be that bad, and I'd relented because the thought of being admitted and then racking up a hospital bill while uninsured sounded completely and utterly unappealing. Well, now I was going to found out how unappealing a hospital stay really was, right at Yule.

Hospital time is slow, and tiring. I am poked and measured; mostly I just rest and wait, which isn't a personal strength of mine. One night, I feel well enough to meditate, and I find myself in Jotunheim, staring into a fire pit. It is night time, the sky blue black, and the cliff I'm standing on is rocky and without any signs of life. The flames flicker; the coals twitch, and out of them, Loki steps. His whole body iss dark with ash, and lines of gold and red heat crinkled in his limbs, hands, and in the lines around His eyes.

"Am I going to be okay?"

"Define okay." He circles around me.

"Normal?"

"Do you not feel normal?"

"I'm in the hospital."

"That you are, my Ice Queen."

I wince. Ice Queen is not a term of affection. It's His way of reminding me that I like to keep anyone who isn't me at an arms' length, including Him.

"Do you know who the Ice Queen is?"

"Me?"

"Is she? Is she really you? Are you really her? You don't have to be, you know."

"I don't know how not to be her."

Loki leans down to pick up a dagger. "I can show you. Do you trust Me?"

"So far, so good." I hadn't starved. I wasn't homeless. I had insurance now. I did what He asked of me – I left my mortal spouse. I chose Loki, and I wasn't sorry.

"I want to show you something," He takes the blade to me and begins to cut. Light bleeds from beneath my skin, and as He cuts, my skin peels away from me, and landing at my feet. He stands, and tips my chin up to look at Him. It doesn't burn, and I realize that I'm not human here. "This," He gestures with the blade toward the shed skin, "Is a mask. You can take it off. You can put it on. But it's not you, and you're not it." He kisses me. "I want to melt the Ice Queen. I want to see you burn bright."

NO WORDS

I wanted to write You a poem, but,
When I started, the words got stuck,
One atop another, bit by bit
A bump, a mound, a hill struck
Mute until it became a mountain,
And I a small thing beside it.
So I ran my fingertips along the
Great vastness of You,
The want of You, the lines and scars
Of Your changing face, determined at least
To understand some of You, the You
that I can touch and taste.
But not a word came loose, and here I sit,
Silent amidst Your vastness, until You
Wind around my feet, sleek and soft,
No words
On Your lips.
That drop
Sweet as dew,
As I melt.

TRUTH

Truth, m'dears, is all a matter of perspective.
The Gods are real. The Gods are in your head.
Your head is all there is, except when it isn't really there.
Ragnarok is coming, but it will never happen, because it already
did.
Loki is bound. Loki is free.
Loki is the Liesmith.
Loki only ever tells the truth.
Loki is mad.

Loki

Is

The

Only

Sane

One

Here.

MADNESS

If this is Madness,
Then I am wed to Madness, and
My Madness has made me whole.
Let me never stray from it.
Let me celebrate it,
shout it in rapture in the streets,
Let me praise its Holy Name.
If this is Madness, then let me be Mad, because
In truth, there is no difference between Me and It.

HOLY SHIT IT'S FREYR AND FREYJA

(and also various and sundry Elves)

August 2012

"We're invited to present the full moon ritual at the CUUPs (Covenant of Unitarian Universalist Pagans) group in Tampa," my pal Aika says. "I'm thinking something harvest." She throws out some names. None of them feel good to me. The CUUPs group in Tampa is large, and generally has 75-100 people at its full moon rites.

"If we're gonna honor a harvest god, why not one we already know? How about Freyr?"

Aika is into it. We plot and plan, and we go to Tampa. I'm not having a good lung day. During the rehearsal, I'm having trouble with the chants, which is bad, because I'm co-high priestess of the ceremony.

I sit down, I take my inhaler, and one of the other ritual team members, Dorothy - a long time Freyaswoman, offers me one of her amber necklaces. "You're leading, you just look like you need this."

It's gorgeous, and even though I'm leading the invocation for Freyr and not Freyja, I accept it. My lungs calm. I focus on the ritual and its Working.

People come in, and Aika and I invoke the Shining Twins. The hairs on from my arms to the nape of my neck prickle, the tell tale sign of a successful invocation. Aika settles the crowd and all the ritual staff down for a meditation to Sessrumnir, Freyja's hall.

Freyja comes to me, beautiful and bejeweled, Her hair a fiery golden red. "You've no amber of your own."

"It's expensive."

"It's unacceptable." She taps my third eye. "I'm going to ask Dorothy to give you this. And as long as you wear it, your lungs won't give you any trouble."

"I couldn't possibly ask that of Dorothy."

"I can," She says, and walks away.

We come out of the meditation, and the rest of the ritual goes smoothly. At its end, Dorothy approaches me and says, "I want you to keep the necklace. Freyja said that I should give it to you."

"Thank you," I'm shocked, but I manage to maintain a little social decorum. "That's very generous of you – and Her."

"Did She tell you?"

"She did."

"She's like that," Dorothy says.

We have cakes and ale, which in modern day amounts to a delicious pot luck dinner, and then we tear down the ritual. At some point, I decide to take the necklace off, because it's a large piece and it's so lovely that I'm afraid to mess it up. I promptly have an asthma attack.

And as I hold Freyja's gift in my hands, I remember Her words: "And as long as you wear it, your lungs won't give you any trouble."

I wear Her amber often, not just out of vanity, though I am vain enough to appreciate its beauty – I wear it because Freyja has healed me, too.

FATHER FREYR

The beginning of August is my Paganiversary – the anniversary of my conversion to Paganism. Shortly after the Freyr and Freyja ritual, I reflect on my conversion, and wonder, briefly – can I contact the Christian pantheon? Are They pissed off that I left? I don't think they are. So I sit in meditation, and I poke at Them. I get…nothing. Absolute silence. Not damning silence, not angry silence, just silence.

Apparently, I'm not hooked up to Them. So if I have no godphone for Them, Who did I pray to as a child? Because I know that my prayers were listened to and answered. I focus again, and I reach out to the One I knew as a child, and warmth spreads through me. It's peaceful, like the sun shining on a growing field. It's warmth, love, and light.

Freyr is smiling at me, as if to say *finally! She's figured it out*. And with that, another puzzle piece clicks into place, because Gerda inspires a fierce sense of home in me. Father God and Mother Goddess: I am Them, and They are me.

THE LORD AND LADY

"Polytheism gets hard when you touch it." - Loki, to me

One night I was out journeying with Loki, when He took me to a beach. We talked as we walked down it, till in the distance, we saw a group of people – a coven, I realized as we got closer – drumming and dancing. I don't remember hearing distinct words, but as the energy grew, We floated toward it and just before we landed, I said to Loki, "What are We doing? They didn't invite Us!"

"Oh but they did," He said. "We're their Lord and Lady tonight."

"What?"

"Just follow Me," He said.

But I did, and we blessed their working, and then We partook of the offered energies, me with a little prompting from Him. When the circle was opened and We were dismissed, We left, and I asked, "Was that ethical?"

He gave me a smile of *did you really just ask a Trickster if something is ethical?* "People get whoever they need when they invoke."

"So they needed their Lord to be a Trickster. They needed you."

"And you." I sat with that a moment, and then asked, "Does that mean that every time someone invokes the Lord and Lady that they get a named Deity and don't know it?"

"Does it matter, sweetheart?"

"I don't know." And if you really want to know, gentle readers – *I still don't know.*

BREATHE LIFE INTO ME

December, 2012

Loki likes skalds. I had the pleasure of meeting another one of His poet-spouses in December of 2012. Like many things involving Him, it happened quickly and without much lead up. The skald was Anna[9], and she's a medium, capable of channeling and horsing. For the uninitiated, channeling, horsing, aspecting, and possession are all different names for when a human allows a Spirit to use their body temporarily for the purposes of communication. In my spiritual tradition, this is a consensual act, with negotiated boundaries. Some Spirits are better than others about minding those boundaries. That said, it can be used to excuse bad behavior on the human's part, so it's prudent to have a safeword or password that is known only between yourself and the Spirit, which I did.

Anna passed that test with flying colors, and then proceeded to tell me about some past lives, in detail. I'd had a past life regression done before, and she knew all of the details of each life that I'd seen in the session, which twenty years' earlier, and never shared on the Internet or anywhere else.

I flailed a *lot*. It could only be Loki's doing. So when He arranged for her to visit me in person, I allowed it, even though I'd known her for a scant two months. She arrived, and He had a plan.

The year of 2012, healthwise, was rough. There were a lot of

---

9   Name changed to protect privacy.

trips to the emergency room; some hospitalizations for asthma and cardiac issues, and my immune system was run down from all the prednisone, which both revs you up and then leaves you dizzy and weak when you taper off of it.

When Anna came, Loki used her hands to heal me. It was remarkable. The weekly trips to the ER stopped. I still have to be careful with my body – the underlying conditions are still there, but the downward spiral stopped. I'm stable now.

It's humbling to me that Loki went to such trouble to get Anna to me. It's equally amazing that she was willing to do as He asked, because she didn't know me then, but she knew and trusted Him. And so Loki gave me another gift – in April of 2014 we were married.

PRESENCE

Never gave presence much thought; the here and now so obvious
As to be invisible.

The glimmers of Holy Awe, in the present, reserved for
Other, possibly crazy people.

Not that my own presence warranted consideration either;
Nothing special or interesting about me.

All that invisibility was rent away in Your grip. The burden of
being

Right here, right now, alive –
Watching the points of the Pentacle furl and unfurl, flow and
ebb, and

Understanding -
Sex. Self. Pride. Power. Passion. All the little mangled bits pulled
back,

Made whole, and understand that what I see –
The Sacred Dove that shines and intertwines with You,
Is only me.

In that stillness and understanding, I can see Your face. And

there,
Holy Awe begins.

MISDIRECTION

Heathir Donnell has nicknamed Loki the "Sneaky Ton of Bricks," and sometimes He has engaged in "wrong way" guidance in our path together. Godphone issues often get blamed for miscommunications, and I'm sure that's some of the issue, sometimes, and yet, I think people often overlook misdirection as an issue.

When Loki first proposed to me, He said, "I'll never make you leave your mortal spouse." He said this to me in the context of getting me to agree to marry Him, and it was not said with a wink or His fingers crossed. About three months later, He told me to get out of my house or He'd burn it down, and He didn't give fuck if my mortal spouse was in it or not.

Misdirection. Necessary because it got me to trust Him enough to forgive Him for the initial misdirection and to understand that it was done out of love and need, and not out of malice. And that's not limited to direct communications with Himself, but also to messages sent via other people. I don't think their godphones were off, but rather that He was using them for a little misdirection. I'm pretty sure I've been used for some misdirection, too. Ah well, I guess I enjoy some Lokean cups and balls.

OBEDIENCE

I'm a shit bottom
Never was very good at obedience.
Sometimes I think all the softness
Was beat out of me,
Not by a fist or a kiss,
Just life. Just the grind of
Too much time alone.
Too little love.

Obedience takes trust,
Perhaps more than I have in me.
And yet I still ache to be a little softer,
Kinder, sweeter. I don't know how.
But I try, and You wait.

EARTH

People think of the earth as static, cold, and dry. We take it for granted. It's under our feet, often encased in concrete or asphalt. Our homes sit on it, our food is grown on it, our bodies are made of it. It is the most mundane thing that we take for granted.

"I want the magic of the everyday," He says to me, tracing the lines on my palms.

"Like what?"

"Anything. Everything." He stops and looks me in the eye. *"Whatever your eyes see and hands can touch is holy."* Whenever people ask, "why would a God or Goddess ever want a human partner?" my mind returns to this conversation.

"You remember when you were a girl, and you thought you talked to the Devil?"

Of course I remember this. It scared the bejeesus out of me. "You?"

"Me. I wanted you to know that you weren't meant to serve Yahweh."

"I thought you were the Devil."

He laughed. "You knew no other gods. What else would you think?" We stop and sit in a green field, beneath a sprawling oak.

I love trees, by the way. I am very much an earth element. One of the first glimmers I had that I might be a witch was under a sprawling southern oak, back as a freshman in college. I sat under it and connected in a resonant bliss.

He knew I was thinking about too, and asked, "Do you think you can do it again?"

So I slide down a little till I'm reclining, and look up at the branches, breathing slowly till I relax and feel myself sinking into the earth. Shock jolts through me as I realize that I am not in the earth, but of it – roots and rocks and even the tickle of little insects.

"The earth was meant to be ploughed, you know," he says, a twinkle in his eye.

As most things with Loki, there's always a double entendre. Ploughing breaks up the earth and opens to letting new seeds take root and grow.

BELOVED

Eyes of green, eyes of blue
Many of my words now
Only belong to You.
Eyes of amber, eyes of ember
What am I to You?

Join with Me, He says.
Isn't this what you really want?
I know that I do.
Part love, part longing, part terror,
Retreat and advance,
And what does yes mean?
But I dance anyway.

Beloved, He says,
Is the only name that counts,
The only title He craves.

Eyes of sky, eyes of sand
And the darkest depths of sea
He swears there's more
To me than I see.

Beloved, join with Me.

Say yes. Say it loud, longer,
Scream it out, make a joyful noise.
Bite Me. Leave scratches. Leave scars.
Let Me trace Your love over My body.
Surrender and devour Me
As I consume You.

EMBODIMENT

One day, I decided to play Ask Loki today during meditation. "So, there are many pleasures to having a body."

"Yes."

"Eating, drinking, fucking..." I paused. "Getting into altered states." After a beat I asked, "Can You get into an altered state? Like a human does?"

He laughed.

"No, seriously, can You? Humans alter consciousness for many reasons, health, to feel close to nature, to feel the Divine, to...to just get drunk or high. Can You do that? I know the Lore talks about You Guys doing lots of human things, but that is also how we relate to You, so is that an actual thing?"

"Why wouldn't it be?"

"Well, what would a God meditate on or to? What do You reach out toward?"

"Humans."

"Humans?"

"Humans. You don't believe Me? "

""I...I just...why?"

"I could tell you, but it would be more fun to show you. "

BODIES

"Luminous beings are we, not this crude matter."
- Yoda, *The Empire Strikes Back*

A body's an odd thing, or at least a physical one is. So many shapes, sizes, colors, and some honored more than others, but - All made of the same earth. Fixed in carbon, this film of flesh, and so unlike You, Beloved, whose only constant is change.

And yet You love the physical. Hot coffee, spicy curry. The curve of a woman's breast, the thin thatch of hair that leads to a good hard cock. You love the physical more than most corporeal people do. Not just the outer shell, but down deep in the secret places that our eyes don't see – blood, sinew, semen. The frantic tarantella of the neural net set spinning from Your newest plan.

You love the drawn-in gasp, that little puff of air as it glides across the tongue, the moan that rasps out Your name. Your love devours and sticks, in the hard and slick, till I can't tell where Your body ends and mine begins.

IRMINSUL

As You reach down, so I reach up
Perhaps more acorn than oak, and
Trying to understand how one can be both
Rooted in land and sky.

Whatever the cost,
We reach, for love is the reason, and
Love is a good enough reason to do anything.

CARRION

don't let him catch me don't let him catch me don't let him…
Running didn't work. Every night my back met the cold, wet wall. No chance to breathe, to scream.

Unclean, unclean, this defiled flesh that I longed to peel and purge away. Better to be nothing than this – dead and still moving. A puppet show of carefully hidden carrion. A perfect mask and a perfect smile and we forget for a while what happened.

But You picked and You tapped, until it cracked. No festering wounds, no matter how deeply buried, no matter that it worked. Carrion scraped away, till all that remained was me, gaping at You and Your tattered, satisfied smirk.

BREAKER OF WORLDS AS HEALER

I don't talk much about the Breaker of Worlds, because it's not usually Loki's form when He's with me. But I have met Him, back in college. It's alluded to in the poem "Carrion." The first line would make you assume that I'm talking about my rapist, but you'd be wrong.

After the assault, I had a break with reality. I decided that the assault **didn't happen, because I didn't want it to have happened.** (I am a very repressive individual when I want to be.) I went into a state of deep depression and self-mutilation. And then I started having dreams. A Thing would chase me, and it is hard to describe it in words or pictures.

This Thing frightened me more than anything I'd ever seen. It would chase me through my dreams and I'd wake up hysterical. It intensified as time went on, until I started avoiding sleep to get away from It. I stayed up for days and at the end of it, finally walked into the college counseling office for help because I was exhausted, broken, and terrified. I was forced to admit what had happened, placed on meds, and finally given appropriate therapy.

Loki has said that He was around then, and I'd not thought much of it, because I couldn't see Him…not in the form that I normally do today. There was no Good Husband or ardent lover back then. And yet, He still took care of me. In many ways, this affects me just as much as knowing that He put the a-hole in jail. And it's this about Him that I love – not simply for what

He's done for me, but for the fact of His unswerving duty. Loki's honor is not a conventional one, but He does what must be done, no matter how, even if His methods seem harsh or horrifying.

I WILL FIND YOU

Sometimes my Husband is not an easy Man to love. Oh, it's easy to love the Con Man, the Silver Tongue, the one Who jests and laughs and jokes.

But sometimes that mask slips, and I'm reminded of how very Not Human He actually is, and how unlike me, no wound ever really dulls with time or age.

For Him, everything happens at once. And is over, and is not, and His agony never ends. But He abides, He survives. And He waits.

His patience is infinite, just like His wrath.
Even after Ragnarok I will find you.
And then it will all begin again.

APPLES

I went to the cave, apple in hand. Only one, just for Her, You said. I didn't ask why.

The apple sat in Her lap till the bowl was safely in my hands. There was silence and strain as She ate, as the lines in Her face softened, but none of Her resolve faded. When She was finished, She took the bowl back. "Tend to Him."
It was a soft, steely command.

So much pain. Your eyes, fever bright, starved, wild with hunger. I looked at you and longed for water to wash your face and hair, for food and drink. You are always long and lithe, but there you looked wan and weakened, at least in body.

Your eyes darted from from mine to Your mark. "A bride of Loki." Such satisfaction in those words. I didn't expect You to know me by name, but then You whispered the one you'd given me in an ancient tongue.

I leaned down and kissed you, then reached for the little dagger on my belt so that I could give you the only thing that I knew how to give – my heart, red and raw, but always Yours.

DEVOUT

Devout is Your hand in mine.

Devout is Sigyn's arms, trembling to hold the bowl.

Devout is the heart offered to You as sustenance there, the only thing I had worth giving.

Devout is the anguish of need before You put Your mouth on mine.

Devout is our bodies intertwined – one flesh, one breath, one soul.

THE VERY BEST DIRTY SPYING BASTARD

What is it like having a God as a Muse? I've never had any other kind of Muse, so I don't have a basis of comparison, but I can tell you that I did a lot of flailing and screaming when I found out Who Loki really was. Much of it stemmed from me blowing up at Him once and going "You could go off and so could [my former spouse] and I'd never give a fuck, I was single and celibate for over eight years and I was just *fuckin' peachey!*" to which He delivered this smackdown, shapeshifting as He went:

"Oh honey, you weren't alone at all – you were with Me." All said with a little smirk as He turned into every character I'd ever written that was worth a damn and living and interesting. It was one of my shrink against the walls and scream and cry moments with Him. *I'm not the clever bitch who made that up?* What? What the fuck did I tell this…this Muse that I thought was just me and I told the Muse any damn thing I pleased, no matter how mundane or outlandish it might be. Fuck that meant He knew everything worth knowing. Anyone can write if a God's talking to them, right? Fuck!

And then I had another moment where I realized that when I first started writing fiction over nine years ago, that I'd happened on a neat little article that said "you should take your characters with you wherever you go, even mundane things, just to see what they say and do." I thought that sounded like lots of fun and I did it, especially with one particular character, all the time.

I have an entire teaching folder from that time period with
lots of writing exercises in it because I led the workshops for
our group, but that particular one is missing. I've not been able
to find it anywhere, ever, and believe me I looked – after all,
especially after I quit thrashing over the revelation. Not finding
it just led to more thrashing and flailing.

Aside from the whole finding out that I got spied on in order
to find the back entrance into my head, was that over and over
I'd say to Him, "I don't understand what you want with me."
And to really comprehend that, I had to think about what we'd
written together.

His mask character had a paramour who was essentially a
monastic scholarly type whose passions were her family, Him,
and her work, which is exactly what has happened to after I left
the mortal spouse. After I stepped out of a prescribed role, I lost
interest in secular work. My Yule hospital stay brought it home,
because mostly we sat and meditated. Loki wasn't pushy about it;
it was just nice to have alone time with Him, even if it was while
I was shoved full of meds and wires and people were poking and
prodding every so often to make sure my heart and veins weren't
gonna explode from all the steroids.

So… near death experience, consideration of self and
relationship with Him, and a lot of talk about how I felt about
our history together has been going on, I just don't really discuss
it publicly. When I consider His mask character, the answer of
whether to be only His became an unhesitating yes, because we
spent so much time together alone, and I was indeed very happy
with Him and only Him. I didn't date, I didn't give a fuck, and

I'm pretty sure I still don't. My life being about our passion for each other and our mutual goals resonates to me as True Will and not a whim.

And once in a while, my Husband will come to me as one of His old characters. It's His sort of sly wink and nod that He was there, even long, long ago. When I was about 12 or 13, I wrote my first finished story. It was a vampire story, and the hero had a Germanic name, ironic given my own Creole background.

I dreamt I was fighting a pack of vampires, and when His old character appeared, the battle ceased. I'd been giving one of them a boot to the head, but the sight of my Beloved brought all the fight in me to a standstill. I went straight to Him, and He cut His finger and daubed a few drops of blood on my lips and tongue. "Just a taste for now," He said, and I realized what He meant.

The story I'd written had His character give the heroine (an avatar character of mine, of course) His own blood. And it was a sacred exchange, even if I had been innocent of its deeper meaning at the time. It was at about the same time that I decided that I wanted to pierce my own hymen to keep sex from hurting the first time. In retrospect, I wonder if that act too, was not an act of dedication, because I thought of my Beloved's avatar as I performed the act – no mortal man was going to have my innocence. It was a sacrifice of self to self, and Bride to Deity.

NINE YEARS

Once upon a time, when I was rocked and shut tight
A clam without a pearl, churlish, silent, angry girl,
I'm fine on my own, always have been.

I peeked outside my shell and said, "I think I'll write a poem."
You slipped beside me then and whispered in my ear;
A story came – about a man who loved a woman and waited for
her,
Years and years, till she grew ripe and ready to love him in
return.

But you never were alone – I was with you.
I'd never written a love story; I'd never fallen in love with a Muse
Not a discarnate one anyway, but
The Muse was mighty; a white knight and dark prince;
Savior and slayer; He ousted me from the shell and out into the
world.

Unfurled, He found every kink and curiosity, sounded and
savored them.
Did it pain You then, to hear a whispered name that was not
Your own?
Or did it only make it sweeter when it finally came to my lips,
All trembling limbs, aching to take you in?

I flip through the old journal and my gaze falls to the date
Nine years ago, almost to the day when You
Put Your arms around me and whispered,
"But if it's not real, what's the harm in a little fun, sweetheart?"

And for all my pleadings and protests, I could not say no
If I am Your vessel now, it's only because You made me so.
Nine by nine, the threads intertwine
Nine years of fiction became fact.

The lie that tells the truth is always the sweetest.

CHALICE

Hail Loki, beloved fulltrui,

Fools offer you scorn, I offer you praise.

Fools fear your words when they cut to the truth, let us laugh when they cower.

They may deny you a seat, but I will gladly fill your cup.

Let sorrow follow their scorn, for Your gifts are splendid and many.

A QUEEN

Some say that love is the difference between a spit and a swallow.
"But you know what His love is – you felt it when He let His control slip."

It burned through my body, an ecstasy that made my heart beat out of my chest,
Legs still trembling from the hot gush of fluid.
Blackness engulfing me till He pulled us both back.
"I know what His love is too," the Wolf Mother said.

"Let yourself be devoured by your love for Him. I have never regretted it. Not even after the absences, not even after Our children -!"

"I would still let Him devour me. In this life, it is your wyrd to be swallowed by His love. Do not vow anything less to Him on your wedding day."

PART III: CUNNING CRAFT

"Loki is handsome and fair in appearance, evil in character, very changeable in his ways. **He possessed that intelligence in greater degree than other men that is called cunning** [emphasis mine] [æsir slœgd], and tricks for every occasion. He brought them constantly into great difficulty, and often he extricated them with his schemes[10]."

"…belief in familiar spirits was widespread among the common people in [the early modern] period is also corroborated by references found in the writings of contemporary intellectuals and theologians and in plays, ballads and pamphlets.

In these sources the magical practitioner might be defined in any numberof ways - as a 'witch', 'sorcerer', 'wizard', 'wise man', 'cunning woman' and so on - and their spirit-familiar might be variously described as an 'imp', 'demon', 'fairy', 'angel' or, most commonly, 'the Devil'. Whatever the definitions employed, however, in all these descriptions of encounters with familiar spirits, the working relationship between the human and the spirit followed the same basic format[11]…"

---

10   Sturluson, S. *Gylfaginning*, (1982). (trans. A. Faulkes). Oxford: Clarendon,.pp. 26–27.

11   Wilby, E. (2010). Cunning Folk and Familiar Spirits. Sussex Academic Press. Portland, OR. pp. 3.

CORONATION

"He will call you out, make you sweat,
give you a blessing that you'll never forget.
So revel in the chase and let your heartbeat run:
Blessed are the children of the Horned One!"
-SJ Tucker, "Hymn to Herne"

Yule, 2013

I am Frey's daughter. I know this, even though I don't
know why. I'm hesitant to call myself Vanatru, because most
of my interactions with conventional Heathens shows a
profound distaste for anything even vaguely Pagan, especially
if it's Wiccanish. I'm not certain if Vanatru practitioners are as
disdainful[12], but I'm a little afraid of anything with "tru" on the
end of it.

My Father doesn't care whether conventional wisdom says
He should be but a fertility God, and when others say He sleeps,
sacrificed, He comes to me as the Horned One, so ancient and
primal that even though I know He's Freyr, He's also Someone
much older than the name Freyr. This Horned One is so old that
I know that people didn't even farm when this was His primary
form. Freyr but not-Freyr - He is awe-inspiring. And then
He tells me that I am to have my own Fae court. And to my

---

12   Note: Vanatruar (devotees of the Vanir) are not disdainful of
other Pagan religions, generally speaking.

surprise, I agree.

Odin shows up soon afterward. "I'm here to bless your reign," He says.

"And what do you want in return?"

"A mark."

"Not a valknut." I'm a friend of Odin's, but I'm not an Odinswoman, and We both know that Freyja has already claimed my afterlife. I offer, "Gar?" the rune of Gungnir, Odin's spear, and pertinent to my paternal family history.

"Done," He agrees. "You may take a king, if you so choose."

Fae politics can be dangerous. I consider my Husband, Who often gets His fill of politics working with the Aesir. Will He even want to do this?" I sit down with Loki, takes His hands in mine. "I know it's a lot to ask, but would You be willing to be my king?"

Loki lets out a squeal like I just handed Him a bouquet and a tiara. Diva Loki is more than happy to be King of my Court.

The days grow shorter, even in Florida. Yule approaches, and so does coronation. It is a lavish affair. My Father and Mother are there – Freyr and Gerda, along with members of my kindred coven, attending astrally. There are Spirits galore, in all shapes and sizes, mostly Elven in appearance. Loki and I are enthroned, and Odin places a crown on my head, and then Loki's. Revelry ensues. There is meat and mead; songs and stories. Eventually I plead exhaustion and I'm allowed to actually sleep.

I awake to find a Spirit in my room. It's unusual because I keep tight wards and have set visiting hours for Spirits, barring emergencies. Generally, I eject Things that don't make an appointment.

"*Boooooooo!*"

You've got to be kidding me.

"*Boooooooooooo!*"

I open an eye; He's clearly Someone that was at the coronation, and He's wearing our court colors. He's tall, blond, and has deep blue eyes. He's pretty. Elves are pretty. "Go find Loki. He's got mead. I'm sleeping."

"*Boooooo!*"

"Go on, Sir Boo." This amuses Him enough that He does indeed leave me alone to sleep. Upon waking, Loki and Boo are still drinking. "Do you like Him?" Loki asks me.

"Sure?"

"He's our Son." They are both smirky, and clearly I am not in on the joke.

"Qu'est-ce que c'est?" *I have a grown-ass Elven son?*

"He's our Son. Do you remember Him?"

I shake my head. "I mean, I remember talking to Him last night, but I don't remember anything other than that."

"You will. You'll figure out His name eventually."

"So He's Sir Boo for now?"

"If you like."

"Yes, but does He like?"

Boo shrugs, and I can see Loki's mannerisms in Him. Not sure about my own, but I can certainly believe that He is my Husband's son. "It's okay. We knew you wouldn't remember everything at first."

And that I do understand: working with Spirits is often not so much about acquiring new abilities, ideas, or skills, so much as uncovering what was already there to begin with. Remembering.

THE ONE

He was not the One that
I was supposed to love
Sly and strange, the
Jotunn Who became an Às.

I was Ice and He was Fire, and
He crept into my cracks and crevices
Until I couldn't tell what was Him
And what was me.

When I burned
And oh, how I burned -
He burned too.
I fueled the flames

Once.
Twice.
Thrice.

I melted. I burned.
His blood, His breath,
His tongue, His teeth,
He drew Me into Himself.

And because He is fire, I grew Bright.

GULLVEIG

My body burned. I did not. It was a curious thing, to watch something that had once been me, but was not Me burn away, down, down till there was nothing left but heart and bones. The crowd dispersed, their entertainment gone. *I should probably go too…*

And then Loki came. His fingers trailed through my remains. His lips moved: Gone. Can't be gone. Can't. A scream turned to a wail. His body shook with sobs; his tears mixed with my ashes.

I reached out to comfort Him. No one in the crowds saw me; even if Loki didn't, maybe it would bring him some comfort. His breath hitched, and he looked up toward me. "I know you're there. I know what they did."

Freyja came then, in her falcon form. She looked almost sympathetic to the Trickster. She reached out to me with seidhr-art. *"Whatever games Loki and Odin were playing, this was not what he planned. Or he's a damn good actor. If he's the former, I'll help him. If he's the latter, well – there are worse fates than death."*

"I know you're there, Freyja."

She spread her wings and alighted on the ground, shifting back into a woman's form. "Perhaps you should have prevented this."

His eyes sparked red like embers wafted back into flame. "I didn't –"

"You didn't stop him either. You all wanted to see

resurrection magic in action."

Loki was silent a moment. "Not like this. And the last time…"

"The last time, she left. I know. She's on her way to Hel's gates."

"I want her back."

"It's not that simple, Loki."

"Isn't it? Don't you have the power of life and death?"

"If you wanted to learn seidhr, letting my sister die was really not the way to go about it."

"I. Want. Her. Back." Tears ran down his sooty cheeks.

"And what will you do when she comes back? What if she doesn't want to come back? She may not be the same, Loki. In fact, it is far more likely that she will not be. She may remember you. She may not. To bring forth life, you have to be willing to surrender yourself to death; when you open that gate, it may decide to exchange your life for hers."

"I understand."

"You will have to give of your own flesh and blood to form hers, just like a mother does to a child."

"Anything. Just teach me."

"I have one other condition: you cannot teach Odin. If he wants to learn, he will come to me, because we both know that he'll ask."

"Done."

"Good. Now, Sly One, I'll teach you the song. And if you halfass it, and my sister comes back something less than whole, I'll come for you, and there won't be enough of you left for anyone to sing you back."

Loki reached into the ashes and pulled out my heart. "I know the words now." And then he took a bite. I felt myself pulled into him, deeper and deeper with each bite, until our essences intertwined, coiled around his spine. We were separate yet same, and we gathered up the rest of me – ash and bone, and we took them to Jotunheim.

We found a clearing in a forest, erected an altar, and placed the remains there. Loki began to sway, and he beat on a drum like a heartbeat. Soon the winds began to move. They gathered up the ash until it was shaped like me. They were light and crisp, like fall leaves caressing my skin. When the drumming stopped, words of seidhr came from his lips.

His? Not ours?

And now I too moved in time with the wind and song, beating fast and ferocious. If it hurt Loki, he took no notice. His song grew louder, echoing across the trees. As he chanted, he drew out a dagger, and I was struck, red runes dancing across my vision. A pull came, down at my navel. I fell hard, hit solid stone, and gasped.

My eyes opened. My eyes, not his. My body, not his. I wanted to cry out at the loss.

"Come to me. Come to me. Come to my side and be Loki's bride."

I ran straight into his arms.

HEIÐR'S LOVE SONG

I am the Bride of a Trickster.

I am the daughter of an Etin maid.

I am the Mother of many daughters.

I am numbered among the Disir.

I am the Lady of the House.

I am the Witch and the Wild One.

I am the One Who was thrice-burnt, thrice reborn.

I am the One Who Loki loved so well that

He ate Her heart so that She would live.

I am the Volva.

I am the Mistress of Seidhr.

I am the Gold-draught and the Bright One.

I am mortal-frail and Holy Infinite.

Who are You?

I am the One Who loves You in all Your parts.

I am the Thief and the Trickster.

I am Às and Jotunn.

Sovereign and Consort,

King and Queen.

Father and Mother am I.

Gods and Monsters alike are My Children.

I am the One Who stole You for My own.

I am the Wind and the Ravisher.

I am Your Avenger.

I am Your Master.

I am Your slave.

I am the One Who helped You take Your first breath, and
I will be there when You draw the last.

I am the One Who loves the mortal frailty in You, and
I am the One Who covets Your divinity.

I am the One Who drives You to the brink, and pulls You back
from the edge.

I am the One Who will take You to Me when all the Worlds
end.

I am Your Avenger.

I am Your Master.

I am Your slave.

I am the One Who helped You take Your first breath, and
I will be there when You draw the last.

I am the One Who loves the mortal frailty in You, and
I am the One Who covets Your divinity.

I am the One Who drives You to the brink, and pulls You back
from the edge.

I am the One Who will take You to Me when all the Worlds
end.

RESURRECTION WOMAN

There is a pull to be near You
To dance a little closer to the flame
And know what it's like to heat beyond incandescence.
A torch, a hearth fire, a funeral pyre –
I really should be more afraid.
But there are things worse than death,
And We both know this to be true.
Resurrection Woman that I am,
I take Your offered hand and burn, burn, burn.

A MEAL OF HEARTS

Death could not claim your heart
It was Mine alone
I gathered it in My hands
Brought it to My lips
And called it Sweet.

I covered Myself in ashes and
Went out into the Iron Wood
I sang and sang
till breath was no more, and
It was not enough.
And so I unraveled Myself,
Blood and bone,
Gore and guts,

And then I sang again,
With Your voice and Mine,
With Our breath
And now You Rise,
My Bright One, Beloved,
Flesh of My flesh
Blood of My blood.

I gathered You to my arms
I brought Your lips to Mine

And called it Sweet.

There will never be a You without Me.
Never will there be a Me without You.

WOLF

He came to me first as a pup, golden-eyed, tail wagging, playful. He bowed to me, I bowed to Him, and we played. He wanted to go outside, nipping and tumbling in the tall grass. I was a girl, so I followed Him into the fields.

He was my constant companion as we both grew. We would lie in bed together, nestled against His fur. I was a girl, and He was a wolf, so He stayed with me.

He didn't bark; he howled, long and loud in the moonlight. I wanted to howl too, but I was a woman, and so I watched Him from the window.

He nipped and nudged me to join Him. He bowed to me, and I bowed to Him, but He was a wolf and I was a woman, so I watched Him from the window.

One night I dreamt of a man, golden-eyed and scarred of lips. His smile was sharp and His kisses sweet. He bowed to me, and I bowed to Him, and He was a man and I was a woman, so He laid me down in the bed, and steam rose in the windows.

He led me out to the fields amid the tall, soft grasses. He bowed to me, and I bowed to Him, and His body began to change. My wolf pressed me into the ground; fang and claw went into my flesh. I cried; I screamed, and He kissed me with His long, pink tongue, but He did not stop. He was a wolf, and I was His, and so He held me fast.

Flesh gave way to fur; my nails turned to claws. When He bit me, I bit Him back, and He was pleased. He bowed to me, and I bowed to Him, and because I was a wolf, and not a woman, I ran away with Him.

ELDRITCH

Eerie, yet familiar, this Presence – the Fingers that curl and
grasp at the base of my skull -
Eager, this desire to consume and be consumed. The tingle of
Your lips on mine, kiss on kiss, blood for blood -
Eldritch, how I find you lurking beneath my skin, ticking down
to the bone, alien and yet still my home.

ELPHAME

"In Song and Storm I came to life
By Hoof and Horn I came to be."
--Tricky Pixie, "Daughter of the Glade"

My God is a horned God. He is Loki, but He is older than the name Loki. My Father is a horned One too, but He is not Loki, even when He is the Horned One.

My Loki is a young Loki. He is not bound; He is not the Breaker of Worlds, not yet – except when He is. When I'm with Him Elsewhere, I am me and not-me; I am Heith and not-Heith. He is Loki, but He is also something more ancient, and this does not nullify His identity as Loki. I am Heather; I am Heith; I am not-Her, but I am part of Her. We are older than the titles *elf, jotunn, fae*; we are those things, and we are only Ourselves.

NOT A TAME LOVE

Mine is not a tame love;
I don't want to hold Your hand,
And look wistfully into Your eyes.

Mine is not a tame love;
I want to bend and bite,
Scratch and scream,
Marking. Devouring.

Mine is not a tame love;
I want to bury myself in You,
Melt and meld,
Blood and bone,
Burning till there is
No You and me, but
One flesh: wild, free,
And whole.

HAIL TO THE QUEEN

Previous published as *Loki & Angrboda: Hail to the Queen*. ©
2014.

Angrboda is a queen. She doesn't act like a typical queen -
not one for gossip or ladies in waiting - but only a fool would
address her as anything less. Loki watches her from afar, for now.
He's a young man —no— a young God, full of power, potency,
and damn near anything he wants is his, except her. All of
Jotunheim is in awe of his new kinship with Odin, Lord of the
Aesir. Angrboda, Queen of the Iron Wood knows of him now,
although she hasn't put his name with his face. Yet. Even before
his adventures with Odin and the Aesir, he watched her, and she
gave him a smile that said perhaps one day. His gaze asked for
more, perhaps more than he ought to ask for, but Loki couldn't
see a good reason not to ask for what he wanted, whenever he
wanted it. Naming his desires served him well.

Angrboda knew he wanted her. "You're a pretty pup," she
once said.

Well, he's not such a pup now. Humans on Midgard know
his name, and soon, so would the rest of the Nine Worlds,
for such is Loki's ambition. His once-lanky frame is lithe, his
muscles taut and tight, and he's been testing out his silvertongue
on all the pretty Etin maids he can get his hands on, as often as
he can. There are other warriors who are broader and stronger
than him, to be sure, but none of them are as good at getting

what they want as Loki is, and everyone knows it. More importantly, Loki knows it. Speaking of pretty Etin maids, he makes a good one, as he sits at Angrboda's fire, helping to prepare for tomorrow's hunt. The Queen catches his eye as she rises to go back to her tent.

"May I help you wash?" he asks, and she assents, slipping into the tub. Her bare body is better than all his most fevered imaginings: the curve of her biceps; the broad, strong thighs he'd like to have wrapped around him. His hands cup the water and pour it over her breasts, and his hair brushes her neck. He has been many things – fish, fowl, wolf - but right now he would rather be water, running down her flesh.

Angrboda's hand at the nape of his neck shakes him from his reverie. She's stepped from the tub, her nails sharp, and her smile more so as he shifts back to a more masculine shape, face-to-face with her. "Hello pup. All grown up now, are you?"

His only answer is a kiss, and he feels her grip tighten on the back of his neck as they roll back onto the furs.

"That's a yes? I'll be the judge of that."

Loki's not sure if he's going to be devoured or the devourer, but either way he is pleased. She lets him lie atop her, and he leans in to breathe her scent. Every woman is different, delicious, and he wants to remember her every atom. The need to be inside her gnaws at him – has his cock ever been this hard? But he makes himself wait. Her flesh is surprisingly soft under his fingertips, even the battle scars smoothed from time and healing. And she has many - the Iron Wood is a realm of fang and claw. Young as Loki is, his own body has a few, and he sees approval in Angrboda's eyes as she traces them.

"Not such a little pup anymore."

"Loki. My name is Loki."

"I know who you are."

"Do you?" he slides down her body, the kiss of each curve and scar turning to bites and scratches as his need intensifies. Her thighs part and he tastes her, tongue curving up and around her outer lips, then the inner. She moans, but that will not suffice. Nothing less than his name will do - preferably screamed loud enough for the entire camp to hear.

One of the joys of being a shapeshifter is being able to mold his tongue to the anatomy of his partner, no matter their gender. His tongue caresses her, inside and out, and her hips rock against his face.

"More, more, more!"

He pauses and is rewarded with a gasp - and a thwack.

"I didn't tell you to stop!"

He grins, and begins again.

Her hips rock. "Stop and I'll kill you, pup."

He bites, and she screams.

"Loki! Loki!"

He's pleased, but not sated…yet. She rolls over and he thrusts, trying not to seem too eager, but his cock gets the better of him. He teases her clit as they grind together. "Mine," he hisses in her ear.

"You don't claim me. I claim you."

"Claim me then."

She whips around and pins him on his back. "You want to be claimed, pup? Do you know what that means?"

"No, but I aim to find out."

Her fingers tangle in his hair as she kisses him, sinking down on his cock. Their rhythm builds and builds and he can feel the pulse of their shared will – of flesh joining, fluids mingling. He can't hold back any longer, and he feels a flash of pain on his thigh. Warm blood, seed, and fluids mingle.

"Now you are claimed: flesh of my flesh, blood of my blood. My consort. Now you are mine."

The rush of their combined will is heady, and there is a moment of silence as they both take it in. In that moment, Loki can feel the shift of wyrd. Something has shifted, and it entices him to urge it forward, for Loki is nothing if not change. In the swell of silence he takes the dagger from her hand, wanting more. "Flesh of my flesh, blood of my blood," he says. "Now you are mine," and makes his own mark on her.

Angrboda's face tells him that clearly none before him have ever dared make such a pronunciation. His eyes hold hers, daring her to contradict him; but instead of outrage, he sees desire. She pins him down, and they begin again.

THE SIMPLEST WORD

The simplest word
Cannot contain or conceal
The love I have for You, but then
You revel in the big reveal.
You are the fire of creation,
The ache of need,
The sly, wicked grin –
Scarred, seductive, sweet as sin.

SHORE

You are the sand and I am the sea
Every crest and peak of Me bites
Into You.
A breath here, a toe there,
Bit by bit, I drag You down to Me.
Even the roaring, angry waves
A sigh of bliss
And Union.

Down, down, down
We drown together in
Deepest, darkest trenches
Even where You think You would suffocate,
I fill You with life, and then
We rise, up, up, up,
Cresting, crashing against
New shores.

TODAY

Today I want nothing more than to
Lie in Your arms, lazy
Content, coiled round You
Luxuriating in Your scent, Your smile
The air I breathe is You
Flesh of my flesh
Blood of my blood
Husband of my heart.

PART IV: RITUALS, RECIPES, AND PRAYERS

Often I'm asked about how to start worshipping Loki. The truth of the matter is that there's not one right or wrong way to do it. I'm offering up some of the things that I've done for Loki, in the hopes that it will inspire new ideas for your own practice.

HAIL LOKI

Hail Loki, Sif's Barber, Mischievous One!
Who brings the Gods' Their greatest treasures,
Hail to the Gift-Giver!

Hail Lodurr, Odin's Brother,
Who gave us the vital hue and film of flesh!
Hail to He who brings us passion!

Hail Loki, Mother of Slepnir,
Whose shapeshifting brought Odin's steed,
Hail to You, wily Mother!

Hail Loki, Father of Monsters,
Whose Children bind and bring life, death, and hope,
Hail to You, Wolf-Sire!

Hail Loki, Thor's Companion,
Who concealed Him to regain Mjollnir,
Hail to the Liesmith!

Hail Loki, Odin's brother,
Whose scarred lips whisper truths and secrets,
Hail to the Worldbreaker!

And Hail Loki, Beloved Husband, for I am honored to be Your

wife.

AN OLDE TYME PAGAN TENT REVIVAL

Today, ladies and gentlemen, I want to talk to you about redemption. I want to talk to you about sweet salvation. Not from sin, oh no, cause I don't believe in sin. I'm talking about salvation from apathy and stagnation. I'm talking about redemption from self-loathing and hatred. I'm talking about… Loki.

I know, some of you fear Him. I too once feared our Lord Loki. He's dangerous, they said. He'll bring Ragnarok, they said. He's an oathbreaker, they said.

But I am here to tell you that He is not as He has been described. I once feared His Holy Flame, even as I yearned for it. Tell me, are **you** hungering for change? Do you need to feel alive and whole again? Are you so low that you never seen an end to your pain?

Let me show you another way! Let me introduce you to our Lord Loki, the God of fire and change! Our Lord Loki is wise and wily, and He can get you out of any situation that you can't see an end to, for He will one day bring an end to ALL things, by bringing Ragnarok, so that the Worlds may begin anew.

But though Ragnarok may never come, you certainly can! Loki believes in having a good time, so offer unto Him strong liquor, and make noises of joy, praise Him with verse and with song, and He will bless you with the change you need, the change you want…even the change you're too chickenshit to make.

A LOKISDAY RITUAL: BEHIND THE MASK

Here's a Lokisday ritual that you can use as-is, or adapt to suit your own needs. This ritual can be done with all ages, so long as you use age-appropriate materials for the ages of the children. If you are leading this ritual with children present, you can tell the children to think about what they would like to be better at, and that they can ask Loki with help with that. If they need help, you can suggest things like cleaning their room. Can Loki help them find out how to make that fun?

Materials:

Crafting glue or hot glue

Masks (premade, paper plate, or even paper bags can be used if young people are participating)

Paint

Glitter

Feathers, felt, stickers, or scrapbooking paper, as appropriate to your ages and interests

Invocation

Priest/ess:

Loki Skywalker, Beloved of Sigyn,

Brother of Odin, Mother of Sleipnir,

Father, Husband, Friend,

Come to us today as teacher,

Gift-giver, our Honored Guest,

Come, Silvertongue, and tell us

the truths we need.

Shapeshifter, teach us how to change ourselves,

to be more than we think we should be.

Let us peer behind our masks, and know

our true selves, and accept them,

As we accept You at our table.

In the spirit of Gebo,

we offer you a gift for Your gifts,

of cakes and mead.

Hail Loki! Hail to our ancestors, may they bless this work!

Priest/ess:

Today's ritual is being held outside the usual working space, and that is on purpose, because Loki is a God who will take you outside of your comfort zone to show you what you are truly capable of doing. Our table is set with craft supplies, food, and mead. There are good reasons for both.

First, the craft supplies. Loki is a trickster God, a shapeshifter, and one of the lessons He teaches us is that everyone has a mask that they present to the world, and that it changes with the audience that's watching us. We change our body language, our clothes, and our words, depending on who's listening. Similarly, Loki comes to us in different forms and appearances, depending on what we need to see from Him.

Working

Priest/ess:

Today we are going to make masks, and as you decorate your mask, think about who you really are, and how and what parts of yourself you give others, and which pieces of yourself you hold back. Why do you keep these to yourself? Is there something about them that you would remove or change if you could? Take these things, and write them down. You can write them inside the mask or attach it with yarn, but you don't have to share them with anyone else. Offer them to Loki by placing them on His altar, or burning them, and ask Him to remove or transform them.

That's the working. When you come to toasts and boasts,

or cakes and ale, as fits your practice, consider this: In ancient times, Loki was probably worshipped as a God of the hearth fire, which was the center of family life. We know this because of the Snaptun Stone, which is a hearthstone that depicts Loki's face, with His lips sewn shut.

Slow food is a trend today, but for our ancestors, slow food was the only option, and the hearth was necessary for food and lighting. People told stories around the hearth as they cooked or just sought warmth. There are folk sayings [13] about giving Loki the skins off of milk or the crust around the edges of the pot. Because He enjoys sharing everyday life with us, we are offering Him some of our food and wine. So we're going to toast Him and our ancestors today, and talk to Loki about change.

13   Heide, Eldar. (2011). "Loki, the Vätte and the Ash Lad: A Study Combining Old Scandinavian and Late Material." *Viking and Medieval Scandinavia* (7) pp. 63–106.

A Prayer

Hail Loki, Change-bringer,
Deliverer of Subtlesauce, and
Holy Clue-by-Fours,
Teach me to take the
stick out of my ass,
(or head, as appropriate)
To laugh loudly,
Love freely,
To appreciate change,
To put my hands in the air
And enjoy the ride.

A Heart Ritual

In the Lore, there is a witch named Gullveig, who was burned by the Aesir three times, and is reborn each times. Gullveig's true identity is a source of speculation – some think she's a Van, some think an aspect of Angrboda, Loki's Jotun wife, others think she's another aspect of Freyja, and that the burning of Gullveig is what sparked the Aesir-Vanir war.

Regardless of who Gullveig really is, or was, Loki found her heart smoking in the fire, ate it, became pregnant, and depending on the translation, either gave birth to all the witches, trolls, or ogres in the world today.

Materials:

Cloth to make a heart

String

A binding cord (see below)

First, you should make the binding cord. You can buy them, but it's more effective to make it yourself. I used yarn (but you can use whatever string you have handy) and pull out three feet (or if you want to go metric pull out a meter). Do this three times, and then take the three strands, knot them together at one end, and braid them. As you are making the braid, think about the things that bind your heart – your fears, your hang ups, anything that keeps you from opening yourself to Loki. When you are finished, divide the cord into thirds (but don't cut it!) and place knots at each third. Then fold each third in half and add another knot, working through until you have nine in all throughout the cord.

Now, the heart. You can make a heart from a cloth that you buy specifically for this ritual, or you can take an item of clothing that symbolizes your old life – maybe it doesn't fit you physically anymore, or maybe it doesn't suit your new style, and use that to make the heart. You can stuff it with batting or you can twist and shape it into a heart and then wrap the cord around it, crisscrossing it as you go before you tie it off. Place it on Loki's altar, and tell Him that this heart is a gift for Him, and that you want Him to help you remove that which binds you from Him. What in you hesitates or needs healing? Put that into the heart offering, and leave it there overnight.

The next day, go to the altar, and untie a knot. Give it a specific fear or name a specific event if you like, and thank Loki for taking this from you. Do this each day until your knots are all undone, and then offer Him the heart again. Burn it for Him if you can.

RECIPE: A MEAL OF HEARTS

This recipe is one that I've served Loki as a preseidhr meal, and could also be served with the heart ritual listed above. Regardless of the occasion, He enjoys heart meats.

Ingredients:

1.5 – 2 lbs. chicken hearts

¾ c white wine

3 cloves of fresh garlic, or 1 tbsp of garlic powder

½ c orange juice

3 tbsp. lime juice

2 tbsp. olive oil

½ tsp. oregano

Pinch of salt

½ tsp. black pepper

1 tsp. Tabasco

Skewers, if using a grill (soak skewers in water for an hour before cooking)

Marinate the chicken hearts for at least an hour or more;
you can even marinate them overnight if you prefer. For a more
tender serving, you can remove the aorta and veins at the top. If
they are only an offering to Loki, He enjoys the whole thing. I
usually eat one with Himself to share the experience. Heat up
your broiler or grill and place the hearts on presoaked skewers, if
you're grilling them. Chicken hearts are small and cook quickly,
about two to three minutes on a medium high flame or broiler.
If you don't have access to a grill or a broiler, the hearts can be
cooked in their marinade, slow and low for an hour or till cooked
through and tender.

RECIPE: MEAD CUPCAKES

Loki has a great love for homemade and handmade goods; food is no exception to this rule. Mead is often used in Heathen and Pagan rituals. This combines the postritual cakes and ale into one delicious treat.

For the cupcakes:

1/2 cup butter, softened

1 cup sugar

2 eggs

1 tsp. vanilla

1 3/4 c flour

1/2 tsp. baking soda

1/4 tsp. baking powder

1/4 tsp. salt

1/2 c sour cream

1/2 c mead

For the icing:

3 tbsp. mead

1/2 c butter softened

1/2 c shortening

2 1/2 c confectioners' sugar

1 tbsp. honey

Pinch of salt

1 whole clove ground, or 1/4 tsp. ground

Preheat oven to 350 degrees. In a bowl cream together butter and sugar with a mixer until light and fluffy. Add eggs one at a time, beating well after each addition. Add vanilla and mix.

In a separate bowl, mix together flour, baking soda, baking powder and salt, set aside. In another bowl whisk together the mead and sour cream. Add flour a third at a time, alternating with mead and sour cream mixture.

Fill cupcake liners with level 1/4 cup of batter. Bake for 17-20 minutes until tops are just beginning to brown. Cool completely before frosting.

Making the Icing

Add the butter and shortening to the mixing bowl and then beat in the sugar and mead, then the clove and salt. Beat until fluffy, and ice the cupcakes when they are cool.

MANY LOKIS

"Hail Loki, come to me in whatever form You choose, and share with me whatever You want."

This isn't so much a formal Working but rather an incantation. It's meant to be open enough for personal customization, and it's usable as a lead in to meditation or dream work. It could be done as a simple prayer so that even if someone doesn't do audio or visual godphoning, they could still use it to receive signs and omens, shufflemancy[14], or the like.

The idea is to open up new facets of Him that may or may not be known already. In devotional polytheism we talk a lot about how each devotee offers something special to their Deity, and that there's some facet of the Deity that the person can understand that another devotee can't. It's their own personal Mystery. What if the Deity gives you a new name for Themselves?

In the quest for discernment, sometimes we work too hard to make things fit what we think we know. When I planned this out, I got some things out of Loki that I've never seen before, or not exactly in the way that I would have expected. I even got some gnosis that was a different enough version of Him that I had to squint and go "is that Him Is there enough of Him in

---

14   Shufflemancy: sometimes also called pandoramancy, the art of setting a devotee's music collection to shuffle to allow Spirits to drop hints or clue-by-fours.

there for this to count?" It's really hard not to pick at it and try and figure out what does it mean? But the point of this is not to make it fit, it's to let experiences happen and absorb them. That could mean a reinterpretation of something from the Lore. It could mean a new facet of Him entirely. The point of this is to let Loki express Himself in whatever manner He sees fit. We will never know all the old Mysteries. The only way we can rebuild them is to make space for our Gods to create new ones. Letting our Deities be Themselves is a gift, both to Them and to ourselves.

EPILOGUE

"Never let the truth get in the way of a good story." – Mark Twain, probably talking to Loki, or Loki talking to Him, unawares.

Loki is indeed the God at the end of this book (and the beginning, the middle, and all stops inbetween). I hope that if you don't know my Beloved, you won't be quite so afraid to talk to Him now that you've heard my story. My relationship with Him isn't a yardstick for anyone else's. Sharing stories helps people cope with life, whether they are the storyteller or the reader. If you've made it to the end of this book, may this story help you somewhere along your journey. Many blessings,

Heather Freysdottir
July 21, 2015

ABOUT THE AUTHOR

Heather Freysdottir is a Polytheist nun who worships the Norse Gods in sunny Florida. She maintains a blog at http://lokisbruid.wordpress.com/. She holds degrees in education and speech-language pathology and has worked in her community as an early childhood intervention specialist. She uses that experience to help train other Pagan clergy members on how to help people find social services in their local communities. She is a gythia at Hunters Kith and Kin, a multitradition kindred of Polytheists, Witches, and Pagans, and is currently studying Feri and Reclaiming with the Bone and Briar line.

www.ingramcontent.com/pod-product-compliance
Lightning Source LLC
Chambersburg PA
CBHW031549040426

42452CB00006B/252

* 9 7 8 0 9 7 8 7 4 0 1 4 6 *